THIS BOOK IS DEDICATED

TO THE

II

First Printing, 2001
Published by Diana Tillion
Printed by A.T. Publishing & Printing, Inc., Anchorage, Alaska

HOMER PIONEERS

Can you imagine how it was
to be these pioneers?
To board a ship to parts unknown,
in spite of family fears.

To sail twenty-five hundred miles
then landing on a beach,
possessions piled beside their feet,
that unknown goal to reach.

From this very stark arrival
the wilderness to break.
A home, a school, a Civic League,
phone system and re-make,

A dock the winter ice destroyed.
And build a few good roads,
the base of what we now enjoy,
that carry every load.

Can you imagine how it was
to be these Pioneers?
Pause for a moment to think,
and in your heart send cheers!

Diana Tillion

AUTHOR'S NOTE

Welcome to the History of the Homer Pioneers. This book is a collection of narratives written by Pioneer family members, and in the case of Ann Sholin and Karl Rosenberg, their own stories. It includes the period from 1896 to 1941 when World War II began, changing everything.

Because Anchorage was such a mad place to live when the war started, my mother and I came to Homer in 1942 on the small vessel St. George (Freddy Svedlund was the deck hand). We rented a cabin from Sam Pratt. I baby-sat the Gordon children. We returned to Anchorage for the school year, then our family moved to Homer in 1943.

We were not Pioneers, but we knew them.

My thanks to those whose stories are relayed and the assistance of friend Marlene Miller, daughter of another Kachemak Bay Pioneer. The gentleman on the cover map is Walt Christensen.

PRELUDE

Sam Pratt, for whom the Pratt Museum in Homer, Alaska, is named, had no children of his own but has an extended family through his sister, Thelma Gordon.

Sam came to Homer in 1935. He spent much of that spring and summer in Seldovia with new friends, Allen and Jetty Peterson. In the fall he came to Homer to work on the fox farm of old Stanton Schaefer, who soon felt too old to manage the farm and put it up for sale. Sam called on his sister and brother-in-law, Thelma and Harris Gordon. On June 23, 1936, Thelma and Harris arrived and agreed to go halves to buy the fox farm. They brought their three little girls with them: twins, Joyce and Joan, and baby Sherry. Sam and the Gordons bought the fox farm from Mr. Schaefer, who then moved into the Harrington cabin. Sam would marry Vega Anderson and build the handsome Pratt House you now see in downtown Homer.

The farm consisted of a small, one-room log cabin with a coal shed built along one side, a barn for the horse, 'Sparkplug', a chicken house, and a meat house for personal game food and food for the foxes.

When Thelma tells of this adventure she smiles like a young girl recalling an adventure that, while not pleasant, was exciting to recall.

"We left Seattle on the Alaska Steamship Yukon for Seward. When we arrived there we were transferred to a freighter half the size of the steamship to be carried around to Seldovia. There we were loaded onto Tom Shelford's little thirty-foot boat to be carried across Kachemak Bay to Homer Slough (now called Beluga Slough) where we, and other passengers and freight, were unloaded and re-loaded into Mrs. Walli's horse and wagon. The ships had gotten smaller and smaller and then to wind up in a wagon pulled by one horse seemed as small as you could get!" She chuckled at the memory.

Their cabin had a little boat stove with a 9" x 13" oven. All the cupboards were made of egg boxes and orange crates, anything that would hold a pot or pan. "Sam knew how I'd feel so he built one cupboard out of beach combed lumber hoping to ease the shock", Thelma recalls. "Harris and I slept in the coal shed with baby Sherry's crib near us and when the wind was bad sometimes the snow would blow in through the cracks and we'd put her in our bed between us," and Thelma would move in the chair as though reaching for the baby and settling it beside her. Harris shrugged. "I never built anything bigger than a dog house. It took me three years to build our new log house."

Sam Pratt and Vega Anderson were married soon after that and they were bunked in the attic of the tiny cabin. During this time a little boy, Galen Gordon, arrived, born in Seldovia. Sam sold his foxes to the Seattle Fur Exchange but the market for fox fur was going out and soon he sold his share of the farm to Harris and went fishing. They estimated there were about six fox farmers left in the area, but even that would soon come to a close. The Gordons would stay there, developing a small farm that provided for much of their needs. After three years Harris, too, got a job fishing with Mae Harrington's father, Mr. Crittenden.

As Homer grew, the children went to school in a little log schoolhouse located where the Junior High is now and roads became a greater and greater necessity. Harris went to work for the Alaska Department of Highways and would continue to work for it under Carl Sholin for the next thirty-five years.

The Gordons have four children, fourteen grandchildren and twenty-three great grandchildren, a total of forty-one extended family members of Sam Pratt who continued his dream of a museum, collecting artifacts and recording Kachemak Bay in oil paintings.

Sam Pratt was an idea man. He was always talking about collecting artifacts, which he did, and of building a museum for historic records. Sam was a fine artist and was a leading advocate of the Homer Civic League, which brought people together to talk about telephones and the dock and other civic needs. Sam worked as the engineer on the Anderson brothers' boat. His reputation of competence in many directions was constantly confirmed.

Sam had the dream of building the museum that bears his name long before it happened. He would donate the land on which it sits. Arleen Kranich would save the minutes of the Civic League and thanks to sons, Bill and Ray, they are included in the Addendum, along with photos from many albums of these great folks.

TABLE OF CONTENTS

INDEX OF PERSONAL NARRATIVES AND PIONEER'S STORIES

Homer Pioneers 3

Lillian Walli 9

Nielsens-Denmark to Homer 19

Ann Sholin, Remembrances of Pioneer Days in Alaska 23

Roland Lee 35

Bert Hansen family 37

LaRene (Tepa) Rogers 41

Gus Anderson and Nils Svedlund 45

Karl Rosenburg 47

Christiansen family 49

Berry's Store 51

Steve Zowistowski's 'Normandy' 52

Joan Gordon 53

Woodman History 63

North to the Future (Edens) 69

History of Arleen and Bob Kranich in Alaska 75

A Tribute to Bob and Arleen Kranich 79

Alfred Jones, The First Fish Plant 81

History of Homer, Tepa Hansen's and Shirley Sholin's Story-1954 . . .83

A Post War Pioneer effort: the Bank of Homer, Natalie Hewlett 93

PHOTOS FROM THEIR ALBUMS 97

1937-1941 MINUTES OF THE HOMER CIVIC LEAGUE 109

INDEX 167

HOMER PIONEERS

Gather 'round here folks and I'll just dredge up a few facts about Homer. I wasn't one of the Pioneers but I knew them. They sure were an industrious group.

Nowadays people don't think of Homer beginning at the end of the Spit, but that's just where it all began.

I just happen to have some old books on the shelf. One of them is GRAMS UNIVERSAL ATLAS, 1899. That triggered my curiosity because Homer was shown in the same size print as Skagway! We all know what a booming place that was. I looked in another book, the "Report to the Governor of the Territory of Alaska" to the Secretary of the Interior, 1901, and learned that the first Postmaster was appointed to Homer in 1896, one Stephen Pemberly. Then checking the first volume of the Harriman Expedition narrative by John Burroughs I found he reported that they anchored off the end of a low sand spit with four or five buildings on it. He was not impressed, stating that "there was nothing 'Humoresque' about the hamlet of Homer," but described at length the grandeur of the Bay and the Inlet.

Then I checked out Dr. Morgan Sherwood's Cook Inlet Collection and

Janet Klein's History of Kachemak Bay and found that what would be Homer began ten years earlier in 1888. Here's a general rundown:

1888   The Alaska Coal Company was founded by J. A. Bradley west of Homer.

1890   An English company opened coalmines at Bluff Point, operating several years, developing a railroad, three mine tunnels,   a roundhouse on Homer Spit, and a half moon dock. This company was closed by an edict of Congress denying foreign entry to mining natural resources.

1894   North Pacific Mining and Transportation Company operated at Eastland, Cottonwood, and McNeil canyons with the Alaska Coal Company.

1896   Homer Pennock, Manager of the Alaska Gold Mining Company, came with a crew of fifty men and one woman, Della Murray Banks. The town of Homer was established, named after Homer Pennock.

1903   The report of the Governor to the Department of Interior said, "...all that we hear of the great deposits of coal in the Southern coast of Alaska, Controllers Bay and Kenai Peninsula is simply astounding. Alaska bids fair to furnish the whole Pacific Coast with an abundance of the highest grade coal for all purposes..."

The coal mining continued, shipping by barge to Seldovia, Anchorage and the Alaska Railroad, as well as the gold mining operations hear Hope.

While coal operations continued at the end of the Spit, people were beginning to move inland. Fox farming was beginning to be a big thing and fish traps were showing up.

1912   When the coal mines in the Matanuska Valley started, the Government closed the Homer mines in support of the Alaska Railroad delivering that coal.

1915   Charley Miller was sent to Homer with 95 horses to winter on Homer Spit for the Alaska Railroad. He homesteaded where Miller's Landing is today. Charley was a wonderful farmer, growing vegetables for the market in Seldovia and for local people, sometimes for money, but not always. He was a generous man and a gentleman who loved to dance.

Homer has had about five distinct eras of dramatic change:

#1   The time of the coaling operation that centered at the end of Homer Spit, with mines to the East and a railroad accessing the ones to the West.

#2   The 20's and 30's, when people came to fox farm and to pan for gold, have fish traps and to farm the land.

#3   The 40's, bringing an airport to Homer because of W.W.II and the subsequent influx of people. Homer was half way to the Kodiak fueling stop for military planes flying to the Aleutians.

#4   The 50's, when the highway pushed through to Seward and to Anchorage, changing Homer's accessibility even more.

#5   And finally the 60's, 70's and 80's, bringing the Oil Boom in Cook Inlet, the fishing boom and tourism. Land's End Hotel, Icicle Seafoods, Northern Enterprises provided the means to make it happen. Homer becomes a bedroom community.

This is a sketchy view of the development in Homer. My purpose here is to speak of the Pioneers - those folks who laid the foundation - just to keep the record straight of whom the key Pioneers were that we have to thank for the good life we have today.

The coal mining industry left no residents. Here are the locations of those mines and the earliest settlers. The winter ice had taken the dock out at the end of Homer Spit and folks were landed off vessels by skiff at Munson's Slough. Their stories follow.

Diana Tillion

A fellow named Rocky Kohler came to homestead and raise cattle in 1900; 15 to 20 head were reported. He ranched for twenty years. A few fox farmers were appearing and fellows were seeking gold by rigging sluice boxes at the stream mouth to the west, like Dick Grey who came in 1912 and settled at the mouth of Diamond Creek. He had a very long rope ladder to climb down the bluff from his cabin. He was a social man, planting a large potato patch and a very large strawberry patch for folks to harvest. A handsome, dignified man seen seated here in the doorway of his cabin.

I can't but think the Wallis were the heart of Homer, as their store was the gathering place for one and all. It provided for the customers, supplies and also provided an area upstairs for dances and other public functions.

This photograph of Homer Cash Store was taken on the Fourth of July, perhaps in 1935. I was told the folks were gathered together for the "women's race".

The photo above is of Ero Walli with daughter Lillian and son Robert.

This photo is of Lillian Walli (Ma to her friends) with the kind expression that always graced her countenance.

Their story is told by daughter Lillian in the following pages.

LILLIAN (WALLI) MILLER

My heartiest appreciation and respect go to the adventuresome and resourceful grandparents and parents and the many others who pioneered the lower Kenai Peninsula and Homer specifically. I will try to recapture their pursuits and experiences as my memory allows.

From hearsay from my people, Minnie, my grandmother, came to America in the late 1800s. She left her homeland, Finland, and migrated across America. Emigrants were pouring in from Europe seeking a new life. The Pacific Northwest seemed to attract many folks. She met and married Henry Linstrang, who was also an immigrant from Finland, and lived in and around the Seattle area. Henry was a veteran of the Spanish American War and had ridden with Teddy Roosevelt and his Rough Riders in that skirmish.

Another venturer, my father Ero, set off to America on the steamship, Lusitania. He was a young man and the year was 1909, and he was leaving his homeland, Finland. His country was experiencing hard times and he was seeking opportunity. He disembarked in New York City and started westward. He worked his way across the country, stopping long enough in each place to replenish his monetary resources, and ended his trek also in the Pacific Northwest.

Seattle was the jumping off place, the gateway to Alaska. Tales of the north country sparked many a young man's desire to seek his fortune there, and Ero proceeded in that direction. He took a job on a fishing boat going north to Alaska, and spent the first summer in Bristol Bay. The next year he got work in the Northwestern Canneries in Kasilof and Kenai. He stayed that year in the Anchor Point area. He lived there a few years and built a number of cabins; a settlement was already there and most likely they helped one another seek shelter.

My father then acquired and operated a fish trap site on the Stariski beach, north of Anchor Point. His friend, Eric Friebrock, who later established the Snug Harbor Packing Co., a cannery on the Illiamna side of Cook Inlet, helped him get started in that venture.

The Admiral Watson steamed into the harbor, Seldovia, its destination. My grandfather Henry, grandmother, Minnie, and their two sons, Edward and Heleki, two daughters, Lillian and Hilya, landed there in 1914. Seldovia was a busy little seaport. The sidewalks, business buildings, canneries, and some of the residential structures were built on piling. The town smelled of seaweed and salt, and one would spot fish swimming under the sidewalk. Fishing boats were tied to docks and canneries; sea birds soared above looking for morsels from the fish processing plants. This seaport remained active through the 1950's and early 1960's.

My people eventually left Seldovia, and ventured north along Cook Inlet. I imagine my grandfather was looking for a way to utilize his skill; he had become a logger. Logs were used in constructing fish traps, and spruce growth grew profusely along the Kenai Peninsula. They put ashore at Stariski, a natural break in the terrain. A river emptied into the Inlet right in front of that valley. The outlet to that river now empties two and half miles further north and parallel to the beach frontage. People that lived in the communities north and south of Stariski knew of each other but distances kept them from dropping in for coffee.

Traveling from one community to another in the early 1900's was no "piece of cake"; some energy had to be expended. Walking was the most obvious and chosen method, with skiing and snow shoeing in the winter. Other methods required the use of our "critter" friends; dog team, horse and cart, horse and sleigh, and finally catch a boat. The boat-on-the-waterways method was by far the most expedient way to transport people and freight, since there were no roads.

After some time, my grandfather left Stariski along with my oldest uncle, Heleki. My grandmother and remaining members of the family stayed and proved up on one hundred and ten acres. My father, Ero, and mother, Lillian, had met by this time and were married in Seldovia in 1919. When my grandmother left Stariski for Anchorage, she left my father and mother the original forty-seven-acre home site and kept the two thirty-acre parcels to the south.

Fish traps had to be a mile from the mouth of a river and the Stariski site met those criteria; my father had the right spot. Most trap sites were owned by interests out of Alaska, mainly the fish barons from the Pacific Northwest. These traps stayed operating until statehood. My late husband Pat and my brother Bob fished that site during the 1950's; our last year to fish was 1958. They were then outlawed because they were too efficient.

My brother Bob was born there on the homestead. According to hearsay, the dentist from Seldovia came there to aid in the delivery. When it was my turn to arrive my mother said "no way" and she went to Anchorage early in the fall of the year by boat. I was born in February; she didn't get back to the home place until late in the spring after most of the ice floated out of Cook Inlet.

The Stariski homestead was a going concern. Four structures clustered together: a bathhouse (sauna), carpenter shop, bunkhouse, a main house and last one to be built. There was a barn, a hay barn, a log chicken coop, and many fox pens built further back into rise in the terrain. The fox pens were made out of chicken wire and anchored down by logs driven three feet into the ground to keep the foxes from digging out. There was a market for furs; they were in fashion then. In the spring when the foxes gave birth to their young, we children had to be quiet: no more hollering back and forth between the beach frontage and living area.

During the summer we had a garden; the vegetables were stored in a root cellar on the side of one of the hills. There was a strawberry patch; in the fall we picked blueberries that grew abundantly back in the forest. Fish and moose were a protein source. We would salt fish for our use and dried the fish for foxes and dogs. There were no convenience or grocery stores nearby so the staple goods were ordered early in the fall from Seldovia. We had storage places and spaces to cache flour, sugar, dried beans, noodles, spaghetti, dried fruit, coffee, tea, chocolate, spices and the like. We had cows, two horses, chickens and an occasional pig. We had milk and eggs most of the time. If a cow went dry we used canned milk that we kept for such an emergency.

My father hired people, especially in the summer, to help with the fish trap operation and farm chores. Some of the folks that lived with us were: Charlie Erikson, a man who could wiggle his ears, which entertained us kids; Karl Rosenburg, who came from the Jesse Lee Home in Seward. Karl worked with us off and on through the years; and went with us to Texas one winter (my late husband and I), and when we lived in the store in Homer, he would help me with my math. George Katchutin was also from the Jesse Lee Home. He was always fun to have around. Charlie Lang, another Alaskan whose family lived in Southeastern Alaska, and John Malaka, a man who came from Poland.

In the summer, on the Fourth of July, some of the tenders (boats that serviced fish traps) would drop anchor and come ashore. We would hoist the American flag and have a party. My father made homemade beer now and again, and us kids would have homemade root beer. Across the river under a windfall, ice was available all summer and we would make ice cream; cows cream and milk was most always plentiful. Everybody would take turns at cranking the ice-cream freezer. Horseshoes was a popular game, and there would be a game a-going. I go there today and can envision those days.

In winter my father delivered mail from Homer on up to Ninilchik, on horseback. "Dickie", his horse that had been shipped from New Mexico was a spirited cow pony. My father had an eager enthusiastic nature as well. An inserted foot in the stirrup would activate the horse to turn toward the rider and off they would go. They were a pair!

My father was a craftsman - a log specialist. He hauled the logs he cut, back in the woods, with his other horse, "Polly". He then peeled and scribed them and hoisted them into position with "ole steady as she goes" Polly, and a come-a-long. Lots of time and energy went into this building project, this last house to be built. How he accomplished the work there on the homestead with the tools that were available still amazes me. He was a musician also; he played the button accordion well. At a social gathering, he would get the party going. In our store in Homer, dances were held periodically, and the polkas and schottisches played on his accordion made the building sway a bit when the dancers got in step.

Homer was a small community back in the 1920's and 1930's. One could count on both hands and feet the families that lived there. We moved there primarily to attend school. The homesteading families were the Glenn Bowers family, Gus Anderson family, Nels Svedlund family, Bert Hansen family, Munson family and Harrington family. Single people were Henry

Ohlsen and Mrs. Woodard (cannot recall her given name), Tom Shelford, Gus Haslund, Bill Peck and his father (whose name escapes me), who was a chiropractor. Over on the east side of town were the Neilsens, Jack Deitz family, the Thurstons, Christensens, Larry Slavin and his father (given name lost from memory) and Charlie Miller. Miller's Landing on the east side is named after Charlie. I'm sure there are other folks I have missed.

Ero purchased one hundred and thirty acres of land from Henry Wells, an earlier homesteader. We lived in the log cabin he built, located on the West Hill Road about five hundred feet from the Sterling Highway, on the west side. My brother and I mushed our two-dog dog team, "Fuzzy and Slim", to school in the winter. We had brought a cow and horse from Stariski and there was a barn and hay barn on the premises. We would then have a supply of milk through most of the winter and my mother would have "Polly" for transportation.

Our school was a yellow one-room clapboard structure that held fifteen or so elementary students. Drinking water was carried from a creek nearby. A coal and wood-burning heater kept us warm. To turn up the thermostat, we students would take turns stoking the fire. Our first grade teacher, Arlene Klockenteger, lived on the premises in a smaller, yellow clapboard structure, about 14' by 16', connected by a boardwalk. Her daughter, Ardis, was our first grade classmate. My other classmates were Shirley Sholin, whom I e-mail often, Bennie Bowers, who drowned, along with his partner "Red" Friemouth, in a winter king crab fishery off the Barren Islands; they lost their lives and I lost a friend. And my third classmate, Esther Munson, who lives in Seward.

Mabel Shotter was our next teacher. She was memorable; she would drive her horse and cart to school the first part of the year and horse and sleigh during the winter portion. She and "Pa" Svedlund would play their musical instruments for the school socials and also for the community get together. Our school Christmas parties were such fun, and the social gatherings brought much pleasure to our small community.

Our closest neighbors were the Harringtons, their land which now is home to the Best Western motel. Mae's father, "Pa" Crittenden gave his adjoining piece of land to the school district; which is located on the corner of Pioneer Avenue and the Bypass road and home of the original yellow school building, subsequently the Driftwood Inn has incorporated that yellow building within it's structural complex. Mae Harrington was our first postmistress and her husband, Bill, was Seldovia's marshal.

We were without health facilities in the early days in our area. Mae's son Jack became sick one fall. He was chosen to walk the beach north to Dick Gray's homestead to bring back some potatoes. He was not dressed properly and caught a cold; it lasted into spring and he was bedridden. Upon arrival of the first steamship he went south and then to Long Beach, where his grandmother lived. He had contracted tuberculosis; he was in and out of the hospital and never did recover. Also Mae's daughter, Jane, had a health problem. She developed an infection on her foot from a blister. According to the story, a doctor in Seldovia amputated her leg above the knee. Generally most of us stayed healthy and that was fortunate.

The Homer Cash Store was built by my father and two other people, "Pa" Svedlund and Dale Pugh, and began its operation in 1934. There were two structures; the warehouse and another building that held the farm feed products, chicken feed and food supplements for the cattle. Our well house contained both the generator for electricity and the well, which supplied our water. The water and electricity we shared with the Shelfords. Tom Shelford and Lydia Reesof were married by then and lived next door. After the Harringtons left Homer, Lydia became our next postmistress.

The Alaska Steamship Co. out of Seattle was the lifeline to what everyone termed as "outside". Their ships serviced the small towns along the Inside Passage, southeastern Alaska, and into the southcentral portion of Alaska. As the country become more populated, they came more often. My father purchased a 1935 Ford half-ton pick-up and a two-ton Chevrolet flatbed. We delivered groceries and hauled our freight from the dock at the end of the spit. Our store was stocked with everything from soup to nuts (both metal kind and vegetable kind). With clothing items, drug products, fresh fruit and vegetables once a month, and groceries, it was an all around general store. A pot-bellied wood and coal heater was first used and was later replaced with a large oil-burning heater. Folks gathered around this energy source in neatly placed captain chairs in the evening and hashed over community affairs. It was a warm friendly meeting site.

The upstairs part of the store was used for social events for quite awhile, until the men, husbands of the Women's Club women, agreed to construct a building for them. And from then on meetings, bazaars, dances and church were held there.

Communication technology allowed us on-the-wall, crank-the-handle-to-make-it-ring type of phones; one short and two longs would get you the Sholins. The store served as the connecting link between the folks in the uplands and the people under the hill and one of us, the operator to push the lever. This phone system was created and maintained by the men of the community and filled a much-needed niche. Homer and Mary High joined our community later and were the founders of a more sophisticated system, a dialing system. We were moving on up!!

The road system back in the 30's and 40's was limited; the road went east to the Thurston's homestead and west to Bidarka Creek, and there were few vehicles. I learned to drive on Tom Shelford's Model T truck. Old "Lena" would shudder and shake when it fired off, but she was dependable. It took two of us to get her going. Wilma, Tom's daughter, would crank and I would manipulate the gas lever on the steering wheel. We never did put her in the ditch! There were two other vehicles in town: Jack Deitz's Model-T dump, and Stanley Neilsen's T model. As new members of the community arrived, they brought their transportation.

The store was in its infancy when my father's health began to fail. I'm sure if he were living today that the outcome would have been different. He suffered a hemorrhage and the blood loss made him very weak. He went to Seward to the hospital; he was given a transfusion, donated by the mayor. He remained in poor health for the rest of the winter, and in the spring he became real ill. Tom Shelford took him on his boat out of the slough to meet another boat that was in transit to Anchorage. A few days later a message came from Anchorage on the radiotelephone stating that he had died; it was June 1937. His body was brought back by boat and he is buried in the Homer downtown cemetery.

Now my mother's responsibilities were many. Being the pioneer spirited woman that she was; she began to use her resourceful nature. She leased the fish trap site to people from Ninilchik and concerned herself with running the business. I always thought the Homer Cash Store was misnamed. Mom's customers earned their livelihood any way they could. Many received their cash seasonally and she would extend credit for months on end. No one went without food; in her spare moments she would bake bread to be sold. At that time there was no bakery, in fact there were no other businesses. The bread was usually given away to whomever. Often, at lunchtime and when she had customers, she would say, "Let's go back in the kitchen and make a pot of coffee." She would then pick up some cheese and lunch meat and proceed back to the kitchen with her customer guests following. Whoever would come in subsequently would be invited also; the community was conditioned for we most always had company at lunch and dinnertime. My mother attracted people; they were comfortable with her. Many little crises were absolved and resolved in "Ma" Walli's kitchen.

My people had a friend, Charlie Sharp, who owned the Seldovia Cash Store. He was a deeply intense, straight-forward and rugged individual. After school, upon opening the store door, the faint scent of cigar smoke told me of his presence. This man helped finance the business; and after the death of my father he came often to give us support. He was totally unaware of the colorful way in which he expressed himself; "hells and damns" were randomly sprinkled within his sentences. During his life in Alaska he invested in downtown Anchorage and Homer property. He later moved to Phoenix and came back in the summers until he sold all his holdings. He was a special person!

Many visitors came to town and stayed with us: salesmen and people from everywhere and Homer did not have a hotel...I sometimes wondered much later how they fared at dinner time, which was my responsibility. We had a wood and coal range; it had to be primed, cajoled, and patted before it performed; however there were no casualties.

Homer was beginning to grow and a new general store and hotel opened. Arthur and Maybelle Berry came from running a lodge somewhere in Alaska to our community. They purchased Henry Ohlsen and Mrs. Woodard's land located in the center of the community. Maybelle had the radio telephone system and kept a schedule connection with Adam Lipke in Seldovia. Also in the 1940's people came to homestead the uplands; some of them were the Heddels—Duncan, Francis, and Peter, their son. Their homestead is directly above what is now the hospital area. Their friends Bill and Helen Wallace, the creators of the Alaska Milepost, lived in Homer seasonally, until they sold to the Alaska Publishing Co. The Lathams and the Herndons were new members of the community, along with many others.

With the advent of new folks many improvements occurred. We had a new school on the hill; Margaret Anderson was their first school teacher. Francis Heddell taught there for awhile and then subsequently in Anchor Point, where they settled in the late 50's. Our downtown was honored with a new school; Lyman and Margaret Allen were the new teachers. This school was a much needed facility; there was inside plumbing!! Our dock on the spit was relocated and maintained; we relied on our dock for our supplies and transportation needs, both the steamship service and smaller boat services.

Heinie Burger and Jack Anderson Sr., competitors, both had boat services between the communities along the coastline on Cook Inlet, and were friends of my people. When "Papa" Jack would dock in Homer, he would come to town and visit. He would relate tales of the rigors of keeping the mail, freight, and passenger service going on the inlet. Jack later purchased two larger vessels and pioneered the tug and barge freight service from Seattle to Anchorage. He and son, Jack Jr., and later his grandson, continued this pursuit until Sealand and then Tote became the major players. Heinie Burger, I believe began the first freight service; my mother told of traveling with him.

World War II began and Alaska became a strategic location, military wise. The Alaska Highway was built in a year by the Corps of Engineers, the military and civilians. Elemendorf Air Force Base and Fort Richardson were established; and the town of Homer was slated for an airport. Stock and Grove were the contractors. It was a wonderful addition to the community; however small floatplanes had already been landing on the slough. Ted Spencer from the Aircraft Museum in Anchorage told me that Woodley Airlines and Star Airlines were present and flying at that time. Woodley Airlines became PNA Airlines and Star Airlines evolved into Alaska Airlines. With the advent of air traffic, came the federal regulatory agency. The FAA, formerly CAA, built a communications building and housing for the operators of the air traffic system.

The Japanese were on the Aleutian chain; they did attack Dutch Harbor and landed and tried to establish a stronghold on the easternmost islands. Jim Arness of Kenai told me of the Harborcraft division of the army that was created to patrol the waters along the coastline of Alaska. He informed me that quite a number of men from Alaska were assigned to that division, because of their knowledge of the Alaska coastline. In Homer [we] were cautioned of the possibility of air raids, and were required to have blackout curtains. We envisioned being invaded and considered our options.

War changed our world and rendered an impact on our community. The military assigned a number of men to the lower Kenai. Our store business began to pick up with all the new activity and my mother enjoyed the challenges. By this time we had a liquor store and a gas station. The oil products came over from Seldovia. I learned to drive our vehicles and became the delivery girl. My friends and I hauled our freight in from the dock. I don't know how we managed all those heavy supplies but somehow we did. My brother had been inducted into the Harborcraft division of the Army, and other young men from our area had already received their respective invitations to serve. We were gaining ground in the Pacific and we Americans had joined our allies in the fight to stop Hitler.

More social activities were occurring with the new population growth, and Pete and Opal James opened a new cafe down on Bunnell Street. Our store seemed to attract social interchanges around the oil-burning stove. I must have improved my cooking skills; we never lacked to dinner guests. My future husband, Pat Miller, would just happen to come by for his groceries about dinnertime. His FAA, formerly CAA, job as traffic controller brought him to Alaska from Virginia; he was an ex-navy communication specialist, and assigned to Alaska.

Many people have implied how fortunate I have been to be the progeny of pioneering people of the last frontier. Many changes have occurred since those people ventured north to carve out a life in this country in the early part of the twentieth century. I have experienced some of those changes with them and now I'm being introduced to the innovations of the later half of the century and into the twenty-first. Yes, I am fortunate! I am a living witness to these folks' unrelenting pursuit of life in this beautiful, yet rugged and unforgiving wilderness. They had the courage, the physical and mental strength, to withstand the isolation and the many hardships along this pathway. My people and their neighbors had the fortitude and patience to stay the course and pave the way for future generations in our north country, Alaska.

NIELSONS - DENMARK TO HOMER

(By Susan Nielson Luzadder)

He almost had it. It was slipping through his fingers. Oh, no! It was gone.

Gone forever to float on the high seas as though no one had ever cared for it. It was his first new hat. His first. Purchased for travel that would take him, his mother, Martha, and six other siblings halfway around the world to a word pronounced Alaska. It was only a word to him now, but it would become the rest of his life.

Years later Karl would be teaching his young daughter the Danish folk song "Little ah Ola" which is about a boy and his favorite red hat. It would remind him of the year 1919 when he was ten years old and standing on the stern of the great steamer looking back toward the distant Denmark. How proud he was wearing his first pair of shoes not made of wood and that new red hat. A gust of wind would change that happiness momentarily. But, he was embarked on a trip with high expectations for the whole family and they would not be disappointed. America would treat them great.

In 1914 Samuel Nielsen and two of his eldest sons, William and Starr, would travel to America. Their destination was Alaska, a place where citizenship meant free land. They would arrive in Homer, build up a farm and send for the rest of the family in five years. The second group of Nielsen children in order of age were Einar, also known as Gus, Peter, Karl, Erna, Frieda and Stanley.

Can you imagine the hardship of a father absent for five years, the long span of time between arriving news? No one would complain as most immigrants they were not a complaining family. They worked the land hard, they worked themselves hard when they fished the bays and farmed the land.

School for the 10-year-old Karl meant starting all over in first grade without much of a command of English. He would learn English but retain a strong Danish accent as a reminder of the family's heritage. Of the two schools in Homer they attended the one-room East End School. The Nielsens consisted of over half of the eight students.

An artist would recreate the scene of the lone homestead at the East End of Kachemak Bay by painting it dusty yellow, with raspberry bushes and a few old cotton wood trees surrounding the house and barns. All is situated on the 160-acre homestead halfway between the bay and the Homer hillside. If you could step into the picture and enter the door you would see first the boys' shoepacks strewn in the hallway. Gazing on into the kitchen, an apron dusted with flour hangs on a hook across from the sprawling enameled green kitchen wood stove. It captures your attention and you wonder how they freighted it from the Homer Spit dock, along the beach, up the bank, through the pastures, and finally to this remote kitchen. How many men and how many horses did it take? Regaining your attention, you notice the house is quiet, as everybody is asleep and probably exhausted from a hard day of cleaning clams and digging potatoes.

Travel was primarily by horse-drawn wagon on the beach when possible, as the tides dictated your schedule. In the winter, it was either skis or snowshoes. Karl was known for his ski trips across the mountains to Seward, staying in cabins along the way. He packed lightly including rice, raisins, sugar and coffee. You could make it anywhere on those staples, at least according to Karl. These excursions were just to deny the winter boredom. Even in Homer, visits would often mean overnighters. And of course there was always walking, actually hiking, as roads were close to non-existent.

Dances were gatherings the locals always looked forward to. Karl would describe these shindigs and conjure up vivid imaginations of farmers and fishermen, mostly of Scandinavian descent, gathering a few times a year and dancing the night away. They had sturdy names like Fred, Gus, Lillian, Vega and Charlie and, of course, the Nielsens. The shy, quiet Karl would have to be coaxed into playing his mandolin along with Brother Stanley on the guitar. As the dance wore on, the hall would probably smell of warm woolen and wood stove.

The fox farm eventually was not profitable and the children went their own way, mostly into the abundant fishing industry. William was killed in a fall from a drilling shaft while working in Seward, Alaska. Starr married and raised his family in California. Einar married Peggy and had one daughter. He worked in a plywood pulp mill for the lumber industry in Washington. Erna married Louis Greenough and raised three boys in Pendleton, Oregon. Louis worked for the railroad. Frieda married Jim Graham who she met in Homer. They moved to Olympia, Washington, had a home right on the coastline. Peter remained a bachelor and lived on the shores of Kachemak Bay and continued to fish the Cook Inlet as a gill-netter. He was known for his clam digging expertise. They say he would have one in the shovel, one in the air and one landing in the coal oil box. They were paid 5 cents a box. Stanley married Eva Branch and also fished the Inlet. They built their home on part of the original homestead. It is still retained by the family as Stanley's granddaughter, Mimi Tolva, now calls it home.

And as you can guess, Karl is my father. I was an only child of him and Mabel, an Eskimo, whom he met in Kotzebue, Alaska while working for the CAA (now known as FAA). There is a cute story I just have to tell in respect to their meeting. Karl was in Kotzebue working on some equipment that was in need of parts flown in. A blizzard was making flights impossible. Unbeknownst to him my mother's sister had it all planned, as they were both single and short in stature. She said "Karl, I have just the person for you." But being a confirmed bachelor of thirty-eight my dad thought light of it. Well, one month later they were married. This was 1946. They teased my dad that he got his parts all right. When they found out Mabel was pregnant they had a house built in Homer. There I had the pleasure of growing up.

I sigh a little bit as I go by our modern Post Office with the paved parking lot, long lines and who knows how many mail boxes. But, the knowledge is inside me of my family of the simpler times in Homer when mail was infrequent and savored.

Thank you for allowing me to bestow a portion
of my father's history with you.

Still a Homerite, Susan Nielsen Luzadder

This photo of Homer dock loaded with sacks of coal, the railroad evident in the foreground, was probably similar to what Samuel Nielsen saw when he arrived in 1914, having come all the way from Denmark to settle on land advertised for homesteading and available for new settlers with lots of energy but little cash.

P.S. Of Samuel's children, Pete would marry a pretty little girl from Ninilchik. Pete's daughter, Carol, would be one of the teachers in the Homer Elementary School. Karl Nielsen's daughter, Susan (Samuel's granddaughter), with her husband, provides a photo shop in Homer and in Seward, and wrote the narrative for the Nielsen family.

D. T.

REMEMBRANCES OF PIONEER DAYS
IN ALASKA – 1925-1969

(By Ann Sholin)

Dear Friends and Family,

I have been sitting here, reminiscing about the many years our family lived in Homer, Alaska; actually over forty years. Somewhat longer than the five years we had planned to stay. I will share some of my memories of these early days in the Alaska wilderness.

I was twenty-four years old when I said good-bye to family and friends in Tacoma, Washington, heading north to be married to the young man Carl Sholin. He had gone to Homer with his uncle Andrew six months earlier. Andrew had come down to Seattle with several crates of live silver foxes and some bundles of beautiful fox pelts, which he was shipping to fur buyers in New York. It didn't take much persuading to convince Carl that Alaska was where to go to seek his fortune. In the early twenties furs were in high fashion and very expensive. Andrew and another uncle, Ed, had been in Alaska since 1912, having signed up in Seattle to work on a sheep ranch in the Aleutians. Neither of them knew a thing about sheep shearing, so were glad when that was over. They liked Alaska and decided to travel to the Kenai Peninsula, where they tried prospecting for gold. Some two years later they journeyed by foot into the Sheep Mountain country. It was here that they noticed many silver foxes. Proceeding on, not knowing just where they were, they decided to mark some trees as they kept moving down to lower levels; thinking there surely must be natives or settlers somewhere. By sheer accident they came into the small village of Homer. It was here that the young men decided to settle. For some time they told no one about the foxes. Eventually sharing their secret with Ero Walli of Stariski, the three built several wooden crates and set off to try to capture some foxes from out of their dens. They were fortunate to get a great many pups. This was the beginning of the fox ranching business that soon spread all over Alaska. A fortune from furs was a short-lived dream. The bottom fell out of that business as the Great Depression neared in the late nineteen-twenties.

Carl wanted me to leave with him (with three days notice). His uncle told us that we could be married by a justice of the peace in Seldovia. I was sure my family wouldn't hear of this. Six months later, much to the dismay of my parents, I sailed north on the steamship Evans, on the twenty-fifth day of August 1925. The trip was pleasant. We stopped at all the towns enroute to Seldovia. There were many adventuresome young people on board, several headed for Seldovia. I was the only passenger going to Homer. I can remember how excited I was when the captain announced that Seldovia was just around the bend. I had told the girls about Carl, how tall and handsome he was. They were all curious to have a look at him. Finally we were at the dock. What a quaint little town, with its boardwalk running along the waterfront. Quite a number of people were milling around, but Carl was nowhere to be seen. I became bewildered and upset. A grizzly, rough looking man with a peg leg came up to me saying he was John Soderburg from Homer. Carl had asked him to meet me and escort me to Shortley's Hotel; the only one in town. He recognized me from a picture Carl had shown him. For some reason Carl, his brother and wife Mickie, Andrew, and some other friends coming for our wedding, couldn't get over on a gas boat until the following day. By this time I was a nervous wreck. I didn't want anything to do with this man, he had obviously been drinking. A kind gentleman off the boat came to my rescue, helped carry my suitcases, and walked me to the hotel. Up in my room I spent some time in tears, wondering what I was doing there.

September third, 1925, our intended wedding day, turned into a nightmare. I became sicker and sicker. Pain in my right side was becoming unbearable, along with awful nausea and vomiting. This is the way Carl found me. No one knew what to do, no hospital or doctor in town. The fishermen were all out herring fishing that fall after salmon season was over. You can be sure we were getting desperate. A big fishing boat loaded down with herring pulled into the dock late that afternoon. They were scheduled to leave shortly for LaTouche. The captain, upon hearing of my plight, consented to take Carl and me aboard, to the Kennecot Copper Mine Hospital located in that town. Some of the men made a stretcher to hoist me onto the boat. I was so sick I wanted to die. I didn't know or care what was going on. Someone put a blanket over me and we were on our way across the Gulf of Alaska. Except for the smell of fish and gas, memory of the trip is non existent. Twenty-seven hours later I was in the operating room, with a ruptured appendix. Truly a miracle, my survival. A month later I was well enough to leave the hospital. It was back to Seldovia on a big freighter, the Northwestern, happy to be alive. Happy also that my family in Tacoma didn't have to know of my close call until it was over. While I was in the hospital, Carl had found a job on a fishing boat. He had good food, a bunk to sleep in, and a small paycheck to help pay the medical expenses.

After recuperating about a week in Homer, we returned to Seldovia and were married on October 15, 1925. My mother had given me a lovely wedding gown, but I wore a simple dress, which seemed more appropriate in a rough-hewn office. I hadn't given much thought as to housing arrangements, other than the fact that we would stay at Andrew's house for awhile. What a house full: There was John, Mickie, their four-year-old son, Billy, and Orma Long (the new Homer teacher). She had nowhere to stay so big hearted Andrew took her in. Orma and I shared a room, with me on a small cot.

Andrew built his own cabin a short distance from the house with an extra bunk for who ever happened along. The main house was large; a coal burning cook stove, and a heating stove were back to back. A large coal bin took up one corner of the living room. Everyone passing by could look right in, as there were no such frills as curtains. It didn't take long for me to make curtains, from sheets - very fashionable today I hear! After Carl and I were married, the living room became our bedroom. A bulky homemade bed took up one corner. I made the mattress out of gunnysacks stuffed with hay (nicely covered however, with sheets). Actually it was very comfortable. Family and friends had given me many sheets, bedding and pillowslips. My dad had made a cedar chest, which was filled with linens. This chest later became a crib for Shirley, our first born child.

Beginning a new life certainly started out with unexpected events! It didn't take long to realize that those who stayed in Alaska were a different breed. Hardships were taken in stride. Making do with what we had and living from scratch made us a creative and strong people. Electricity, running water, stores, mail service - not to mention doctors or dentists - were for city folk. No use for cars; they don't run on trails through the woods.

Washboards worked fine. Stiffly frozen clothes taken from the clothesline in winter smelled so good as they thawed. The worst thing was having to dash to the two-seater outhouse after dark. Bats would swoop down at me, and hoot owls terrified me. Glen and Phina Bowers had the first bathroom. What a treat to just look at such luxury. Phina invited us to take a bath in a real tub anytime. Homer did have something that most other villages did not. A house-to-house, crank telephone system the local men had put up. Every time the phone rang, up went all the receivers. Believe me, there were some hilarious conversations. Everyone in town knew everyone else's business. Andrew's ring was two short and one long ring. The emergency ring was a real long ring. Fires, injuries, even a shooting or two were reported to the townspeople with that system.

In times of sickness we had to depend on our own common sense to know what to do. Fortunately, people didn't get sick very often. Plenty of walking, pure food and clean air had something to do with that. There was no depending on specialists of any kind. Maybe that was good, for all twenty-five original families truly depended on one another in times of need.

In the fall of 1926 a herring company began operating at the end of Homer spit. Some local men were needed to put up cabins and a cookhouse for the crew. Carl hired on to work on these buildings. When the workers arrived form Seattle, Squeaky Anderson, the boss, asked me if I was interested in being the cook's helper. I became a working lady. Local men caught the herring and this saltry crew packed the fish in salt in big barrels, to be shipped to the States. Squeaky liked my cooking and hired me to go to Halibut Cove with Carl and nine other men, where a second herring saltry was begun. A big tent, boarded up five feet, was the cookhouse and our living quarters. The nights were getting chilly. Snow was falling on higher elevations. I recall getting awfully tired of cleaning and cooking fish. The men, mostly Scandinavians, would lay fish on the steps nearly every day. They could eat fish for every meal. The cookhouse was full of good food. How could anyone eat so much fish, I wondered? One morning while I was frying hotcakes, I fainted. Carl picked me up and put me on the bed. In a few minutes I felt all right and went back to cooking breakfast. Those poor guys looked so worried! They thought I had a heart attack. Right then it dawned on me, I must be pregnant! When the camp closed, Squeaky gave Carl and me all the remaining groceries, a wagonload. Best of all, when he learned I was expecting, he gave me a boat fare for a trip home to Tacoma. I went out on the old steamer, Watson, seasick most of the way. This was in March of 1927. Shirley was born at St. Joseph's Hospital June fifth. After three months at Grandma's we returned to Homer. Carl had homesteaded on acreage adjoining Andrew's. Our one-room log cabin was finished. He and

Alfred Anderson dug a well and readied a garden spot with a horse and plow. On the next homestead was the Gus Anderson family, having arrived a few months before we did. They had built a sod house; warm as toast in winter and cool in summer. On the flat roof, pink fireweed blossomed merrily - in season. What a picture that made! They, too, were busy working on their big log house. Another neighbor was the Nels Svedlund family, settling about the same time as the Gus Andersons. Both had school age children.

The first school was a one-room log cabin on the Harrington land, near the beach. Jean Flindahl was the first teacher, with six pupils. She contracted tuberculosis and had to return to the States. Orma Long replaced her. A second school on the East Side, on the old Neilson farm near Millers Landing, had a few more pupils. The teacher was Nellie McCullough.

Events of forty years ago are sometimes hard to pinpoint. Around 1936, Ero and Lilly Walli opened a large general store. Prior to that time, people who could afford to kept extra groceries on hand for those who ran short of necessary food. Fishermen brought groceries and mail over from Seldovia. There were times during fishing season and during stormy winters when we would wait a month for boats to come in. Wallis store had a big oil-burning stove for the men to sit around and chat. Such comfort and congeniality. The upstairs was a big dance hall. Pa Svedlund played a fiddle. That was music enough for the polka, schottische, two-step, fox trot and a waltz or two. Children were brought by their parents. Little ones slept on coats on benches, and older ones soon danced along with their parents and friends. Such fun! I'll never forget the school Christmas plays, presented to applauding parents and friends. These were real productions. Memorization and practice took at least a month. No cue cards, no reading the script, only a whispered reminder by the teacher to those who occasionally forgot a line. The whole community went all out for holidays. When movies began showing in Seldovia we were quite envious. A truly memorable event was when Seldovia people brought an occasional movie over to be shown in Walli's upstairs hall.

Snowfalls were heavier in those days. In the winter whenever we went anywhere, Carl would hitch Nancy, our horse, to the sleigh filled with hay. We would snuggle down in the hay and warm blankets, all tingling with excitement.

There were no such luxuries as school buses. In winter, the children sometimes had a hayride in a dog sled, or they skied; when it was icy they crunched down the road with creepers on their boots. At times in the deep snow, snowshoes were necessary. Other times the children took their sleds, riding down the hills and taking turns pushing one another on flat ground. Rarely did they miss a day of school.

Homer's first post office was at the end of Homer spit. Folks walked, rode horseback. or rode in a wagon for four miles each way. There were times when the scheduled mail boat wouldn't arrive, and the long distance traveled was for nothing. In a few years, Tom and Lydia Shelford had the post office in their home; much handier, especially in winter. When a post office was built, Mrs. Arlene Kranich became postmistress, a position she held for many years.

Very slowly Homer grew. Our two boys were born, both in Uncle Andrew's upstairs. Nellie Munson was a self-taught midwife. She helped deliver Bob in March 1929 and Dale in July 1933. Our second daughter, Lois, was born in Seldovia in December 1939. A doctor delivered her. This was a difficult birth and I nearly didn't survive.

Schoolteachers were looked upon with deep respect. Many of the early day teachers were single young women. Fondly remembered by our family are the Richardson sisters. Margaret arrived in 1929. She taught at the one room, West Side school for a year. In 1930, her sister Marion, who was twenty-four, took her place. Alfred Anderson, a young bachelor who was our close friend from the time we arrived, began courting her. They shared a love of books, politics, walking in the woods, and enjoying the beauty and quietness of that lush country. In 1931 they married. Sister Margaret returned to teach again, while Marion stayed at home enjoying being a housewife. Their first child, a sweet spirited little girl nickname Missy, was born in the summer of 1932. Two years later in July, a second baby girl was delivered in Cordova. In those days, without local facilities, expectant mothers who did not relish the thought of home birthing traveled to larger towns. Since most had no pre-natal care, they had to use their best judgment as to when they thought birth was imminent. Marion chose Cordova, where good friends had urged her to stay with them. Many times it was months away from home, first waiting, then recuperating. Ten days hospitalization was the norm in those times.

Margaret, who had been teaching at Chignik, was again going Stateside. The SS. Starr, which she was leaving on, was due to stop in Seldovia. Marion, who was homesick, decided to take the two little girls to Seldovia to stay with Alfred's sister, Mrs. Lippincot, and await Margaret's arrival. This was October, when storms blew in, making the Inlet a dangerous place for small boats. The SS. Starr was damaged, and beached, making it necessary for Margaret to leave on a different ship which did not stop at Seldovia.

Marion waited for two weeks, not knowing what had happened. Communication was by letter (very unreliable) and she had no word. Finally deciding to return home, the mother and babies boarded a small gas boat for Homer.

There was a big tide running that day. The sea was rough. The men in charge of the boat had a dory in tow, loaded with lumber. Boats were docked in the Slough, and the tide was an important element. If the tide was swiftly going out, and the weather unfavorable, piloting a small boat in was a hazardous proposition. The boat lurched when hit by a big wave, and swamped in minutes. Marion, Missy and baby Aileen were drowned. The two men, Fred Munson and Ed Anderson (no relation to Alfred) were saved. Ed hung on to the mast and was saved by Alfred and Tom Shelford. Fred somehow made it to shore, and had to be packed home. When the tide went out, Missy's body was found in the engine room, and Marion's on the beach towards Homer spit. She was still clutching the baby's blanket in her hand. The baby's body was never found. Alfred had been home that morning, glancing every little while across the bay to see if he could sight the boat. When he saw the little speck across the inlet, he began walking towards the beach. The horror of what happened and the inability to do anything was almost too much for him to bear. Ignoring the dangerous sea, he and Tom Shelford pushed out in a dory and made it to the boat. Reaching down through a skylight, he touched Marion's hair, but rescue was impossible.

Shirley recalls that day, as she sat at her desk in school. The windows faced the water and Munson's son was watching the boat's progress. Suddenly, he jumped up, running for the door, shouting, "the boat swamped!" Teacher and students all ran to the beach. The one long ring on the telephone alerted the townspeople, and soon the whole community gathered and grieved together. When Marion's body was found the next day, Mrs. Groth (who had some knowledge of nursing), Phina Bowers, myself and several other women, washed and prepared Marion's and Missy's bodies for burial. Nothing could have prepared us for such an ordeal. Dick Grey was asked to make the funeral arrangements. The caskets were lovingly crafted by Pa Svedlund. Women of the community made wreaths decorated with homemade, artificial flowers. Three men dug a grave under a giant spruce tree. Mother and daughter were placed to rest in separate white painted caskets. Friends rallied around to comfort Alfred, who was devastated at the loss of his bride and darling babies. He never again lived in his and Marion's cabin, but moved to Margaret's place. Many years later, he remarried, to Carl's sister, Esther, who also was a Homer teacher. Both have since passed away in Portland, Oregon.

I remember many of the bachelors who lived in their little cabins around Homer. Dick Grey, with his shelves of books, settled about twenty miles up the beach near Anchor Point. To get to his house, one had to climb hundreds of feet up a rope ladder, which stretched up a sheer cliff from the beach. There was Dad Shafer, a most kind gentleman, so good to our children. Shirley remembers a beautiful light blue organdy dress that he ordered from Sears for her 12th birthday. Also, one Christmas he gave her a treasured Mickey Mouse wristwatch. Charlie Miller lived on the East Side, with his unmistakable fondness for garlic. Ernest Bird was a jeweler, a quiet man with a photographic memory. "Cat man" Larson, so called because of his hordes of cats, didn't need blankets. Cats covered him at night. If anyone came to the door, cats literally flew in every direction; they were terrified of strangers. He must have spent a fortune on cases of canned milk. "Old Man" Holmes was another unique fellow, who lived with his sister on the East Side. These people were rarely seen. Their cabin was completely filled with cardboard boxes, leaving only narrow alleyways to walk through.

Until Carl and I left Homer in 1969, his work was with the Alaska Road Commission, now the Bureau of Public Roads. Gravel roads were built through town in the thirties. I believe it was Jim Waddell who had the first automobile. Everyone in town had a ride. We lived about six years in Andrew's house. When we moved to our cabin with our growing family, Carl added on a living room, bedroom and bath downstairs, with two bedrooms upstairs.

Since we were centrally located, the road bosses from Anchorage asked me if I would fix their meals. Mr. McCroskey, the first foreman, lived in our rental cabin. He and his wife planted a garden, which they enjoyed immensely. Donald McDonald, later known as the Father of the Alcan Highway, was one of my boarders. When McCroskeys left, Carl became foreman; a position he loved for twenty some years.

How I worked! We had a huge vegetable garden, strawberries and raspberries. I made cottage cheese, churned butter, made all my own bread and pastries. Carl always got his moose, and that had to be canned. It was several years later that we had a refrigerator and freezer. Our root cellar, dug into the hillside, was filled to capacity every fall. Bins heaped high with potatoes, carrots, turnips, rutabagas and cabbage. Shelves were loaded down with jars of berries, canned salmon, moose steaks, meatballs, and mincemeat. Wooden barrels held salt fish. No wonder the men I fed gained weight! We always had a cow or two, chickens, a pig and horse. Besides everything else, there was haying to be done in late summer. Carl built a huge log barn, with its fragrant smelling hayloft where the kids liked to play

- jumping from the rafters into the soft hay.

Shirley left home at age 15 to go to Seldovia for her senior year in high school. She lived with Jack and Susan English. She, too, had a ruptured appendix. This happened in February 1943. Dr. Ralph McKenzie and family had come to Seldovia, where they had charge of the new, small hospital. The good doctor had gone by boat to visit some of the native villages along Cook Inlet. A storm kept him away for two days, while Shirley, packed with ice bags, waited in the hospital. She didn't realize the seriousness of the situation, but I did, remembering my own frightening episode years earlier. This episode became a blessing in disguise, as the McKenzies invited her to spend the remaining months of school with them. Shirley helped with their two children and worked in the hospital doing small jobs. When the doctor made his rounds of home visits, she trudged along with him. He enjoyed teaching medical facts and never forgot to quiz her later. When they left to practice in Anchorage, they took her along and got her a job at the old Providence Hospital. The following year she was accepted in the Cadet Nurse Corps training program at St. Joseph's Hospital in Tacoma; right back where she was born. Nurses who graduated from this program during World War II were obligated to serve in the military. Fortunately, the war ended before she graduated. How sad we were to learn of Dr. McKenzie's death in a small plane crash in Seldovia Bay. After many years in Colorado, he had returned on a vacation to see Seldovia again. Here where he had begun his medical practice, it also ended.

During the Korean War, in 1950, our Bob was drafted into the Army. He was stationed at Fort Richardson in Anchorage. In June of 1951, Shirley and her husband, Dick, with their two small children, came home for a family reunion. Bob was given a week's leave. What a joyous time we had! Our joy turned to unbelievable sorrow upon receiving a telegram from the Army, informing us that Bob was missing and presumed drowned. On the weekend of his return to base, he and Eugene Kranich went fishing at Big Lake. No one witnessed the boating mishap, but the young men didn't return to the dock. The empty boat was located far out on the lake. Carl chartered a small plane and circled around and around the lake, hoping the boys were safe somewhere along the uninhabited shore. It was two months before Bob's body surfaced. Carl's hair turned white almost overnight. During that time, I recall standing in our living room one night, looking out of the window into the blackness. I uttered a little prayer, "Oh God, let me know if Bob is safe." At that moment, the full harvest moon suddenly appeared in an opening in the clouds. It was brilliant; coloring the billowing clouds around it a soft gold. In a few seconds that gorgeous sight was gone. My prayer was answered. It seemed as if God were telling me that Bob was safe in His care.

My terrible grief began to ease.

Dale married the former Helen Elias, from Chinook, Montana in February 1958. Shortly after they moved to Soldotna, where Dale was transferred with the Bureau of Public Roads. He later became foreman there, until he retired in December of 1984. In June 1985, I received the heart-breaking news that he too had drowned. He had taken a friend to their beach place across the bay from Homer. During the night he rowed out to his big boat, to anchor it out further at tide change. As he jumped back in the skiff to return to shore, something happened; again, we will never know what. Alaska waters claimed another son. He left his wife Helen and two children, Steven, age eighteen and Shelley, sixteen. How difficult it is to accept the loss of loved ones before their time. At times like these we learn how fragile life can be, and how important it is that we value our family relationships.

Lois, the last to leave the nest, also went to Tacoma, where she became a nurse. She and her husband, Dale, lived for many years in his hometown of Duluth, Minnesota, where he was on the police force. The Pacific Northwest beckoned them back. Lois now works in a doctor's office in Fife. Their oldest daughter, Teri, is Mrs. Ken Ereth, Diane is in college, and Michael is an eighth grader.

Shirley's two daughters each have three children. Donna and husband Michael Yarbrough live in Fife. Sherry is Mrs. Michael Pasinettti. They live in Milton. Greg, the youngest son, will soon be finished with his training to be a journeyman electrician. He is married to Jan, and has a son. David, Shirley and Dick's oldest son, is the only family member with a full-blown spirit of adventure. He visited Europe, England, the Scandinavian countries, and taught school in Sweden and Guam. For the past three years he has been an English teacher at a university in Japan. His wife, Kazue, helps with private English classes, when she isn't busy with their three children.

At last count, I have nine grandchildren and ten great grandchildren.

Life in Alaska, as a pioneer and sourdough, was good. True, there were hardships and tragedies, but that is a part of living that we all share. Love of that land, with its fine people and its unrivaled beauty and peace will always remain with me.

Our old home was demolished this past summer to make way for a business. I like to remember how beautiful it was, with gardens and flowers, and mostly when family and friends sat around the big table eating, talking, laughing and enjoying one another's company. Alaskans stop by now and then. Ermel Gjosund has made several visits. Lillian Walli Miller spent a few days with Shirley last winter. They grew up like the Bobbsey twins. How good it is to talk about bygone days with old friends. Vilma Matheson, another old timer visited a few weeks ago. Harry and Wilda Hegdahl, who had the first theater in Homer, live in Ashland, Oregon. It has been awhile since they have gotten up here, but we keep in touch.

I am almost eighty-five years young. Carl passed away, unexpectedly, at home in September 1982. Blessed with quite good health, I keep busy with my flowers and keeping my comfortable home. My girls keep watch over me. Shirley has returned from nursing, now spending much time in Christian education of the Methodist Church. I'm content and happy. We raised a good family, doing our best under primitive conditions, in those early days. Looking back, I'm thankful for every year in beautiful Homer, Alaska.

Sincerely,
Ann

Building the road across Beluga Slough, 1927.

Carl Sholin and his Uncle Ed were instrumental in getting the road built across Beluga Slough, which made Homer Spit accessible by road.
The inset photo above is loading gravel off the beach to build the roads.

ROLAND LEE

1923 brought Roland Lee to Alaska. Roland was an Australian who had left his native home because of a family tragedy. He sailed off around the world on a ship, aboard which he was the radio operator. How the ship came to be in Cook Inlet has never been told, although it's logical to speculate that it came to Homer for coal.

During the voyage, Roland had become ill and knowing it was terminal, he asked to be left on the beach. Above the beach he could see that the bluffs were eroding. He was given provisions and left to die. A tragedy to those on board, I'm sure. Roland, like Dick Grey, was a fine gentleman. Interesting to think of them, one ten miles West of Homer and the other ten miles East.

Roland built a little sod hut on the edge of the bank. He constructed a small fish trap to catch fish and crabs to eat. He planned that when his time came the bank and his hut would slough off onto the beach and be consumed by the sea storms.

However, he didn't die. He built a small log cabin farther away from the edge of the bluff. He planted a garden and got to know his neighbors. He rigged a radio with his little set he brought from the ship and with a copper wire, rigged a way to choose stations with a clothespin. People traveling up and down the beach would stop by for tea and those folks he met hiking to town for supplies and mail grew to know him and learn that he could repair radio problems. Eventually he had to build another cabin, plant another garden site and expand his fish trap, as he often gave some of his catch away. Folks would laugh when they told about his sequence of cabins and his strange radio setup, but always with great admiration.

When his time did come, he asked his neighbors to bury him in a shallow grave and seed it with flowers so they would be nourished by his remains. Unfortunately they buried him six feet under, but they did plant the flowers.

D. T.

HISTORY OF BERT HANSEN AND FAMILY (1898 - 1976)

1898   Bert Hansen was born in Harstad, Norway (above the Arctic Circle) on October 25th.

1920   Bert came on the ocean liner Stavangerfjord to the United States in August to Tacoma, Washington, to see his aunt and uncle Giske. He worked halibut fishing.

1921   He moved to Bellingham, Washington.

1922   In the spring he came to Alaska, and worked for Libby McNeil & Libby at Taku Harbor.

In the fall he returned to Washington and went to work for Weyerhaeuser Timber Co. in Everett.

1923   He returned to Alaska and herring fished in Seldovia as skipper on the M.V. Juneau.

1924   He remained as skipper on the M.V. Juneau.

1925   He was the skipper on the Cleveland, fishing herring in Kachemak Bay. There was a saltry on the Homer Spit.

1926   He was the Captain on the M.V. Shaken for Fidalgo Island Packing

Co. in Port Graham. In the non-fishing months he carried coal and freight between Homer and Seldovia on the boat Maybe.

1927   He was the skipper on the General Pershing for Everett Pacific Fisheries.

1928   Bert married Inga Tensvold on October 5th. She was the bookkeeper for Knute Armstrong.

1929   He fished for Pacific American Fisheries with a sailboat in Bristol Bay. He continued for the next 18 years to fish in Bristol Bay in the summer until, in 1947, they changed the fishing to motorized vessels.

Bert and Inga moved to Anchorage and there their first son was born. They named him Gilbert.

In the fall they moved to Seldovia. They went from Anchorage to Seldovia on the M.V. Kasilof.

1930   Inga taught school in Ninilchik for 2 years.

1931   Their first daughter was born September 4th, they named her LaRene Joy, she was nicknamed "Tepa". Bert was given an offer to go to China to teach seining to the Chinese, but he didn't go.

1932   They built a two story log house in Seldovia and then moved it log by log to Homer.

Bert operated a hand trap with Torvald Jensen on Kalgin Island for the A.Y.R.[cannery.]

Bert built a shed behind their house in Homer and opened up a store, hauling the goods and other freight from Seldovia. They sold out the store to Wallis in 1936.

1936   Their second son was born in Seldovia on October 26th. They named him Gerald William. He was nicknamed "Booie".

1941-1944 Bert was Captain on the Ruth L. for the A.Y.R. salmon cannery.

1941-1946 Bert worked as 2nd engineer for Civil Aeronautics, building the Homer airport.

1943   Gilbert, their oldest son, passed away in the Swedish Hospital.

1949-1955 Bert had a hand trap on Kalgin Island which he, Booie, and Tepa operated in the salmon season for Snug Harbor   Packing. He also built hand traps.

1953   On December 11th, Tepa married Lawrence Rogers.

1955   On March 23rd Tepa had Bert and Inga's first grandchild, Linda Mae.

Inga died in the summer while Bert and Booie were fishing the hand trap; she had diabetes and high blood pressure.

In the fall, Bert went back to Norway to visit his mother and sisters and brother.

1956   On June 8th, Tepa had Bert's second grandchild Judy Ann. He was on the Minnie B with his son, Booie, as Captain,   working for Snug Harbor Packing Company.

1958   On February 18th, Tepa had his third grandchild, Anita Mary.

1958-1961 Bert was on the Loon as 1st Mate with Booie as Captain, working for Emard Packing Company.

1961   Bert fished the Violet.

1961-1964 He was the watchman for Whitney Fidalgo in Seward until the 1964 earthquake when his cabin and he floated to sea.   H e then moved to Anchorage.

1965-196_ He worked as night watchman for the railroad.

1975 Bert died in Anchorage in July. He had had a stroke a few years before.

Inga Hansen with their children, Tepa, Gilbert and little Booie.

Gilbert and Tepa playing on a swing.

LARENE (TEPA) ROGERS

I was raised in Homer and lived in the log house, which still remains, just above what is now called Inlet Trading Post on Main Street. Our home, the log house, was originally built across the Bay. It was taken apart, log by log and rafted across the bay to Homer and re-built in its present location.

My dad, Bert Hansen, used his boat, the Maybe to haul passengers and groceries across from Seldovia. A shed was built on our home and used as a grocery store until we sold out to Wallis in 1936.

My Mom, Inga Hansen, was a schoolteacher and also very involved in getting Homer's first library started. She first taught school in Ninilchik and later in Homer. I can remember having my Mother as my teacher when I was in the 5th grade. That was bad enough, but I was the only one in the 5th grade, so learned some from the 4th grade and some from the 6th grade. It all worked out well since we had 4th, 5th, and 6th grades all in one room.

One of my memories of home was washday. I can remember using a washboard and tub, but later we had a gasoline washing machine. The day started early in the morning by carrying water from the creek, then pouring it into a tub on the coal stove to heat. While the water was heating, we carried in the rinse water. When the wash water was finally hot, we carried it by buckets out to the shed where there was a gasoline washing machine. Hopefully the machine would start before the water-cooled. After the clothes were finally washed and rinsed we drained the water into buckets and carried it out to be dumped. Then the clothes were hung out on the line to dry. During the winter the clothes would usually freeze dry or get partially dry so we'd bring them in the house to dry completely.

We always had our own chickens. Another memory is putting the eggs down in a barrel of water glass mixture, a preservative that kept the eggs through the winter months. The worst part was reaching down in the cold slimy mixture to get the eggs when needed. We also raised our own vegetables and had a good root cellar built underground in a hill. It kept the vegetables through the winter. We canned our moose meat and fish, since, of course, we had no electricity for refrigeration. Every fall we ordered our yearly supply of staple groceries.

We had fun times in the winter. The kids would gather in the evening with their sleds. Not everyone had sleds, so several of us would pile on each sled and down the hill we'd go. We would start from Walli's, which is now Nomar Canvas, and go all the way to the beach. Of course the beach was a lot further out than it is now. Then we had the long walk back up the hill, but it was fun. We'd either sing or just talk, but had to keep moving fast just to keep warm. Sometimes we'd all gather out at Beluga Lake for a fun time of ice-skating. Some of the parents would also come and we would have a big bonfire and hot cocoa to keep us warm.

I always enjoyed going down to the beach to get coal. In those early days when there was a lot of coal on the beach, we spent our time throwing it in piles above the high water mark. We would put a stick in the center of each coal pile to designate our coal. Then when the tide was low and we had more time, we'd haul our coal home. That's where I learned to drive, by driving the truck from one coal pile to another.

Dad had the first taxi service. We ended up with two Model A Ford sedans. He seemed to stay fairly busy. Sometimes if he was out and a call came in for taxi service, I would get to take it if it was just around town, even though I was only twelve years old. I still remember our call number was three long rings and two short ones, on the crank telephone.

Another big happening was when the Alaska Steamship came in once a month. The main thing was it brought groceries to both stores. As soon as the trucks brought the items in from the dock, we'd rush to the stores, mainly for fresh fruit. The Alaska Steamship also carried passengers and was a big attraction.

Another important time was when we turned 16 years old we could work in the canneries. We mostly all worked for Snug Harbor Pkg. Co. It was a great time when the cannery tender would come into the dock to pick us up, take us to Snug Harbor, and then a month later return us home. My last years of cannery work was working with Francis Pavaloff at Libby, McNeil & Libby in Kenai.

For several years I worked with my Dad and brother on our hand trap at Kalgin Island. A lot of my time was spent as cook, and I also had a set net to fish.

After graduation I went to Business School in Tacoma, Washington, for one winter and returned home that summer. I drove up the Alaska Highway with my Aunt and Uncle.

I went to work for Wythe & Son Builders, who were also agent for the Alaska Steamship. When Mr. Hewlett opened the Bank of Homer, I went to work there. I worked as a teller, posted statements, and did any other work as needed.

In 1953, I married Lawrence Rogers. He had homesteaded and built a house about 3-1/2 miles west of Homer. The house has been added on to, and we still live at the same location. We have three daughters, Linda, Judy, and Anita. I quit work at the Bank before our first daughter was born. I stayed home and was a mother and housewife until our youngest daughter graduated from High School. I then went to work part time in the kitchen at the Homer Middle School (now Intermediate) and am still working there - ten years later as of 1986.

There have been too many changes over the years to list. Homer just isn't Old Homer anymore.

Tepa Hasen washing clothes on a srub board.

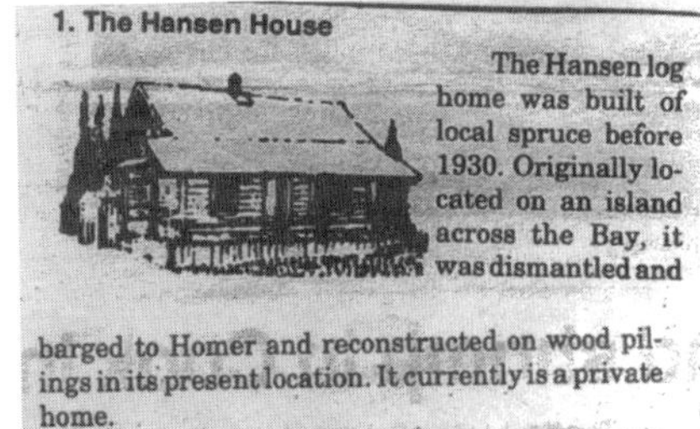

1. The Hansen House

The Hansen log home was built of local spruce before 1930. Originally located on an island across the Bay, it was dismantled and barged to Homer and reconstructed on wood pilings in its present location. It currently is a private home.

On the corner of Bunnell and Main Street is the old Inlet Trading Post, now Bunnell Street Gallery.

GUS ANDERSON AND NILS SVEDLUND

1923 brought Gus and Nils to Seldovia. Alfred Anderson (no relation to Gus) also came to Seldovia in '23. All passengers and freight came to Seldovia by ship and then was transported to Homer in small boats. The winter ice on Kachemak Bay had taken to the dock off the end of Homer Spit, so the small boats would deliver the freight and the passengers to Munson's Slough (later to be called Beluga Slough). Mr. Munson's small boat was the main means of transportation at first, and later, after 1935, Tom Shelford.

The boats would land at the mouth of the Slough where the road reached the beach. There would be a horse and buggy or model T Ford waiting to meet the boat.

In 1933 a terrible tragedy occurred there. The freight boat approached the Slough in heavy seas with Alfred Anderson's wife, Marion, and two little girls aboard. The skipper sent the passengers below so they would be safe from the swells washing across the dock.

An unusually huge swell rose up behind them, capsizing the boat. Those on the shore waiting to meet the boat could hardly believe their eyes. Tom Shelford, who was there to meet the boat and row the passengers ashore, pushed the dory into the hammering seas. He was able to rescue the two men on board but they could not break into the capsized hull of the vessel to get Marion and her little girls. They found Marion in the hull of the boat and

one of the little girls down the beach to the west, but never found the body
of the baby.
D. T.

   Years later, in the 40's, I lived at the top of that beach and on a heavy
Southwest storm Alfred Anderson could be seen walking the beach at half
tide; a heart-rending sight.

D. T.

KARL ROSENBERG'S STORY

(written by Karl Rosenberg)

Karl Rosenberg born September 10, 1914 at Unalaska, Alaska.

My parents died when I was very young. [I] was raised by an orphanage there 'til it was moved to Seward, Alaska, where I finished High School.

Then I moved to Homer, where I worked for a farmer one summer. The next year came to Homer, where I worked for the Walli family on their hand fishtrap.

I went to visit Unalaska, worked on the military base at Dutch Harbor. I was drafted into the military. Spent over 4 years in the army. When I was discharged I came back to Homer. Worked on Mrs Walli's fishtraps for two more seasons.

I then went to work on Fidalgo Island hand traps. The fish traps were [in] three different locations. I was on them 'til they were outlawed.

Me and a partner bought a Bell saw sawmill. We cut more for other people.

Bought a fifty-foot landing craft from a cannery with the stipulation that we fish tender for them for 5 seasons (picked up fish from Moss brother and from your husband [Clem Tillion] on Kachemak Bay).

My partner and I bought a big sawmill after the earthquake. It kept us busy in the fall and winters 'til that land was made into a park. It was too hard to log close enough so we sold the sawmill to a man in Seldovia. Quit tendering in 1970.

Worked as a deckhand for Tom Shelford hauling freight and mail. That was before the dock was built.

Worked for Jess Willard at Caribou Lake in fall season. Went on some of the fall hunts, took care of the horses, took meat and hides back to the lodge.

That is what I remember.

When we moved to Homer, our past California neighbor, Olive Smith, who had taught school at the Unalaska orphanage, wrote to advise us to be sure to meet Karl Rosenberg. He was one of her early students that she still corresponded with, and was so bright and talented.
D. T.

THE CHRISTENSENS

Walt Christensen is the fellow on the cover pointing out the location of Homer on the Gram's Atlas.

The Christensens came to Seldovia in 1932; Walt, his sister, Pearl, and brother, Glenn. They went to school in Seldovia that year. Mrs. Shotter was their teacher. The next year, 1933, they moved to Homer and took out a home site near Charley Miller on what appeared to be a nice flat field. They came in winter and found in the spring it was swampland.

The addition of three children made a count of seven on the East end and a school was set up on the Deitz homestead in the building that many years later became Mickey's Market. Mrs. Nordby was the teacher. Walt and Pearl were in high school and were immediately put to work splitting wood and being janitor. This lasted two years, during which time a road was built between Miller's Landing and the West Side School near the budding town of Homer, and a bus was established to transport the children.

A friend of Jim Waddell from the Jessie Lee Home at Unalaska suggested that a full section of land be let out to farmers to raise money for the Home. Mrs. Christensen filed on 80 acres of that land and they built a fine log home with the help of neighbors, then set about farming. Walt was one of those persons who was always there when needed, always cheerful, always kind. He drove the first mail and freight truck from Homer to Seward when the highway was constructed, serving everyone along the route. At age 85 he was providing food service to the Pioneer Home at Ninilchik.

Mrs. Shotter from Seldovia also filed on a piece of that land. Nils Svedlund had taken quite a shine to the middle-aged widow and proposed marriage. Being the New England lady that she was, having ordered a New England style home to be built in Seldovia, she would only consent to the proposal if Nils would also move her house to Homer. She filed on 80 acres of that land and was a neighbor of the Christensens.

D. T.

Above is a photo taken by Bill Wakeland of the Coal Creek hand trap. Hand traps were privately owned rather than those installed by the canneries. However, the canneries happily purchased their fish. This was becoming a common source of income.

BERRY'S STORE

Another store was established when the Berrys came to Homer from the Interior. It was located south of Hansen's place, where the road turns to go west, and to go on down to the beach and east to Beluga Slough. The building was as large as Walli's store with the store on the main floor, and upstairs were living quarters and rooms to rent. The store was very professional in its merchandise but did not have the charisma of Walli's. The store would be taken over by a man named Bunnell who also came down from the Interior.

During this time, '35 - 40, the fox farming had diminished and the fishing, mostly traps, had increased.

The 1930 census reported Homer having a population of 35 persons.

D. T.

Steve Zowistowski was not a Homer Pioneer, but his little boat, the Normandy, delivered freight, passengers and mail to Homer. Steve built the boat himself. Steve Thurman bought and donated the boat to the Pratt Museum.

JOAN GORDON

The wind was out of the southwest that sunny afternoon. The day was June 23, 1936. The Homer hillsides were a lush green with barely a sign of habitation.

Harris L. Gordon and family were arriving from Playa del Rey, California, to take up fox farming in Homer. The previous year Harris had bought the homestead and fox ranch from Stanton Shaffer, who had proved up on the homestead in 1924. Sam Pratt made the arrangement for Harris.

Harris, Thelma and three children, twins Joan and Joyce, age 3, and Galen, age 16 months, had arrived the day before in Seldovia aboard the SS Curuco from Seward. Seldovia was the shipping center for the area. The Seldovia dock was owned by Juanita Anderson, who was on hand to greet the family as they disembarked.

It had been a long trip thus far, as the family had driven from Southern California to Seattle in their Model A Roadster. After spending a few days with relatives in Bellevue, they set out to sea on the SS Yukon from Seattle for Seward.

The trip up the inside passage was beautiful and the water calm as the ship made its way from one cannery site to the next, dropping off supplies for the summer fishing season.

Now they were on the last leg of the trip. Aboard the gas boat Jungle Queen, owned and piloted by Thomas L. Shelford, they traveled to Homer. Kachemak Bay's afternoon swells were too much for Thelma, who had to sit out on deck and hope for the best. She really couldn't appreciate the beauty of the day and the country. Harris, however, was alive with anticipation and expectation.

This was not the first time for Harris to enter Kachemak Bay. In 1924 he had come to Alaska at the invitation of two cousins, Jettie Peterson and Enid McLane. Harris had just graduated from Seattle's Garfield High School and was looking for adventure and work prior to attending the University of Washington.

Harris spent that fall working herring in Halibut Cove for Charlie Sharp. The first of January that winter of 1925, he hiked the beach from Homer to Kasilof, where he spent the winter with Archie and Enid McLane. McLanes had a fox ranch and farm and Harris spent many hours in the woods hunting for fox feed.

The next summer was again spent in the fishing industry, after which he returned to Seattle and spent one term at the University of Washington. A bout with chicken pox caused him to go to his parents who were now living in Fullerton, California, to recuperate, thus ending his formal education.

Harris got work in the oil fields with Union Oil and worked there for ten years. On a vacation trip with a friend in September 1930, he met Thelma Hope Pratt in Paynesville, Minnesota. After an eight-month courtship by mail, they were married in Thelma's farm home June 8, 1931. They made their home in Ingelwood, California. However, his heart was still in Alaska and he continued working on plans to return.

Thelma had grown up on a Minnesota farm and worked with her parents at their Lake Koronis resort. Having vacationed in California with her parents while in high school, she envisioned marriage as a long and happy life in sunny Southern California. Therefore, she did not view the Alaska plans with much enthusiasm.

At the time of the family's arrival, Homer did not have a dock so they were off-loaded on the beach at the mouth of the slough at high water. Thelma remembers Lydia Shelford, Ann Sholin and Lilli Walli being there to meet the Jungle Queen as the boat brought groceries and mail from Seldovia. Life in Homer had begun.

Of course, the bulk of their belongings could not be transported on the Jungle Queen and had been shipped with Heine Berger on the M/V Kasilof. The boat did not arrive till early fall. Harris later learned that the Model A Ford, with their cooking stove in it, was used part of the summer in the little town of Anchorage for sight seeing till it got dented in some mishap by the "borrower".

Instead of the roadster to transport them to their new home, they went with team and wagon owned by their nearest neighbor, Guy Waddell. West they rode past the little log post office off the beach on the slough side and the Shelford's yellow frame house near it. Their garden on the beach side of the road was growing potatoes and other vegetables.

They rode past the log house of Bud Bernard on the old coal mine railroad bed. They rode past Woodard's green frame house and farm, which Henry Ohlson farmed for Mrs. Woodard. Her husband had disappeared on his way back from Seldovia in a skiff loaded with lumber sometime earlier.

They continued on, past the yellow frame school house and teacherage on the right, where nine students had attended, and which was located on the Crittenden homestead; past the black tar paper shack on the Crittenden homestead, now owned by his daughter, Mae Harrington; past the log house Shaffer had recently built on the Crittenden land by permission of Mae.

Next they went past Ero Walli's log cabin and barn on the right, which were a mile from the post office. This was their winter home so that Bob and Lillian could attend school. Their home and fish trap were at the mouth of Stariski Creek. On the left side of the road below Walli's lived Nimic in a dugout with his rabbit.

They went past Guy Waddell's, which was at the end of the old railroad bed, and now a maintained road, at Bidarka Creek. A quarter of a mile past the old coal shaft hole stood the barn and log cabin, which was to be home.

From the homestead cabin a footpath led on to the slide and down. Mr. Rose had a cabin in a large grove of cottonwood near the beach. Further up the beach Jens Jensen had a cabin on the beach near the lakes. Dick Gray lived in a cabin on up the beach above the bluff and the mouth of Diamond Creek. There was also a cabin at the beach where the man Larson lived with his many cats.

This was near the end of the depression and there were eight to ten men who panned for gold dust along the beach at low water between Homer and Anchor Point. They didn't make much but enough to buy beans and flour to live on. Sam built a sluice box and he and Harris tried their hand at mining for gold at the foot of Bidarka Creek. Not only did they find it hard work shoveling off the gravel and rock to reach hard pan; but after a week, they managed to collect one ounce of fine dust. That was poor pay at $35 an ounce for two men.

Though the cabin that awaited them was one of the better log cabins in Homer, it was a far cry from the house in Playa del Rey. The coal shed was made into a bedroom for the family, as Thelma's brother, Sam, had the loft.

Harris paid $1,500 for the 160 acres that included the fox pens, barn, chicken house, meat house, tool shed and blacksmith shop, large root cellar and cabin. He purchased the cow and calf separately for $100. He had to purchase the telephone in the cabin that belonged to the community phone system for $25. Harris bought the silver fox breeding stock from McLane of Kasilof.

Old Lily, as the cow was called, gave five gallons of milk at a milking twice a day. That surely did help in those lean years. Her calf, Civit, later turned out to be a good milker. Thelma, who had much experience milking cows on the farm in Minnesota as a girl, found milking this cow a different experience as the cow was not used to women and dresses.

They found two horses on the place, Spark Plug, which was retired from the Anchorage Fire Department and was stove up with arthritis, and old Shorty which was being pastured for Mae Harrington who had gone "out-side". After the first year, Spark Plug was replaced with big black Polly, which they got from Ero Walli. Both Shorty and Polly took delight in try-ing to make Thelma's life eventful.

Thelma says, "Old Shorty was a cunning and exceptionally intelligent ani-mal. He was also a leader. One morning when Harris went to feed the foxes he found the potato patch, which had just been weeded and hoed, flattened with some hills completely torn out. Shorty had opened the gate and all the horses had gone in and rolled in the nice soft dirt."

"One day I looked out the window and the horses were looking at the front gate so I watched them. The gate had a piece of one-inch pipe that ran through a hole in the gate and into a hole on the ten-inch post. Shorty nibbled and worked at that pipe for some time to no avail. He turned around and was about to sit on the gate when I opened the door and yelled 'Shorty, stop that'. He turned around and looked at me as much as to say 'What are you so upset about?' and looked only slightly guilty."

"One day Mrs. Berry called and said our horses had visited her strawberry patch. I couldn't believe it for there were the horses on the hillside where they'd been the night before. However, later that day, Mrs. Walli also said she'd had visitors early in the morning. Then I knew Shorty had been at the gates again. Harris went around all the outside gates and drove nails through the boards so Shorty would be too uncomfortable trying to sit hard enough to open the gates."

"Again I had our house garden all in perfect shape and had even taken a picture to send to our families "outside". The next morning, when Harris went out to milk he came back in and told me he had some bad news. Shorty had been up to his old tricks. My beautiful garden was a mess. They had not only rolled in it, they had taken bites out of nearly every head of cabbage and pulled carrots. Then Harris had to pound nails through all the gates inside the property."

"Shorty was so smart that if asked to pull he would lean into the harness; if it didn't move easily, he'd rear up on his hind legs and act like he was really going to try again, but he wouldn't even tighten the tugs. Instead, he just left the pulling to Polly."

That first summer was one to remember. The Gordons arrived during haying season and due to the cook stove not arriving, Thelma had to cook on a 24" by 24" stove, which was her waterloo. Either she would stoke up the fire and burn things or the fire would go out with the bread half-baked. To make matters worse, she had a boil on her right hand, which made any work very painful.

Sam had a garden in but wasn't used to the size things grew in Alaska. The telephone peas he planted grew up the 3-ft. fence and lopped down the other side to the ground. He had canned a dozen quarts of moose meat and had a bumper crop of potatoes.

The prices in Alaska seemed astronomical to Thelma. In California she bought Mannings Best coffee for 18 cents a pound. In Homer, Hills Brothers was 35 cents per pound. The groceries came over from Seldovia and were left on the beach. The canned goods could take it but the flour and sugar suffered. Sometimes only the center of the bag was usable. The eggs!!! Thelma learned in short order never to use an egg without first breaking it into a dish.

They added chickens to their farm when Marion Waddell asked them to take care of her chickens so she could go as cook for the Waddell big game guiding outfit the Fall of '37.

In September of 1936, Sam Pratt and Vega Anderson were married. Now there were two families for the little 16 by 24 cabin, attic and lean-to.

May 20, 1937, the Gordon's youngest child, Sherry, was born in Seldovia after a several week stay at Mrs. Haumelbaucher's home. She was the midwife in the area for many years.

In 1937, Harris and Sam both worked for the Alaska Road Commission for four months, driving truck and hauling gravel. They worked for seventy-five cents an hour that summer. The ARC had three trucks, a crawler tractor and pulled grader. McCrosky was road boss that year. Pete Bagoy followed him as boss. Later Carl Sholin held the position for a number of years. Harris was to work for the road commission, except for five years as a commercial fisherman, till his retirement in 1970.

The days were long and full in those early years in Homer. Thelma remembers hauling 39 pails of water one day with a neck yoke from the spring for family and garden. Wash water was heated on the stove in a tub. Baking bread and churning butter were part of the chores. Also there was the never-ending care of the foxes, from babies to pelts.

Sam snared rabbits for part of the fox feed. One day while checking his snares near the slide he found a cub bear in one. As he went to release the cub the sow popped up over the edge of the bank and Sam made a dash for a tree. The only one handy was an alder. The higher he climbed to get away from mama bear the lower the tree leaned. The only gun Sam carried was a game getter, which shot a .22 and/or a 410 shell. The 410 shell he had with him had been through the wash. Just as the sow stood up to claw him out of the alder, she opened her mouth to roar at him and he shot her in the mouth. She died instantly. Needless to say Sam was still shook up when he got back to the cabin.

One day Harris and Sam butchered a steer and hung the hide on a birch limb at the edge of the woods south of the barn. The next morning the hide was gone. On investigation Sam found it down in the woods in a pocket of alder brush. He dragged it back and put it on the limb deciding a bear hunt was needed.

Harris was stationed in a tree, with Thelma at the foot near the edge of the woods, while Sam and Vega were to make the drive through the woods. It seemed to take a long time, and Thelma walked over to the creek bank and stooped to look under the tree boughs when up popped the bear, right in her face. Her screams sent the bear off, with Harris only seeing the tall grass waving Mr. Bear's good-bye.

Two mornings later the hide was again gone. They revised the original plan, and Harris and Thelma did the driving through the woods while Sam and Vega waited at the clearing for the bear to come out into the open. This time they were successful in their bear hunt.

In 1938 Sam and Vega built a small house on the southeast ten acres of the homestead, where they lived for a couple of years, till they got their house in town built in the early forties.

September 1938, Thelma took the children out to spend the winter with the grandparents in California. The fox fur prices had dropped, but Thelma was able to sell their share of the pelts to family and friends and pay for the medical treatment that was needed. That ended the fox farming. Eventually the farm animals, which had grown to four horses and six head of cattle, would have to go, as Sherry was very allergic to animal dander and hay. She would get asthma even from a person who had been around a horse.

In June of 1939 Thelma and the children returned to Alaska on the SS Cordova. The men of the community had built a dock at the end of the Spit at which the Alaska Steamships now landed. Most of the community took delight in meeting the ships on their monthly trips. As the family was waiting for the baggage, one young stranger came up to Thelma, giving her the once over and said, "So you are the woman I've heard was the best looking and best dressed woman in Homer." Thelma did take some ribbing because of her stylish city hats, and wearing white shoes through the mud to community affairs.

Sam had cut trees on top of the hill in 1935 and skidded them down on the snow where he ricked the logs up to season in anticipation of a larger home for the growing family. Sam also salvaged material from what was left of the coal mining buildings at the end of the Spit after the fire. Harris peeled and slabbed the logs on one side with a broad axe, as time permitted. He started putting up the rounds of logs in the Fall of 1939.

By late fall of 1940 the family moved into the partially completed, ten-room log house. Harris didn't claim to be a carpenter, but Thelma had a nice kitchen with real cupboards and water piped into the house. Eventually the house was completed to stand through the 1964 earthquake. It was there-after torn down and the Farnen home now stands in its place.

Thelma was active in community affairs. She was the first president of the Parent's Club, whose concern was to get a new schoolhouse as the little one-room building was inadequate and very hard to heat. She belonged to the Women's Club. This club held different socials to raise money for commu-nity needs.

She was also concerned with the spiritual needs of the community and says, "When we arrived in Homer we met a family who was associated with the Jesse Lee Home in Seward. They came to Homer to raise a garden to supply vegetables, both fresh and canned, for the Children's Home for win-ter food. The Groths lived about two miles east of the school. They had three children of their own and had brought three of the older boys from the Home to help. Mrs. Groth and I decided we needed a Sunday School for the children and any others of the small community that could attend." From that start eventually came the first church in Homer - the Christian Community Church.

In 1941 Harris drove a truck, hauling gravel for the building of the airport. The gravel was hauled off the beach from near Munson's Point. Babe Gray was killed on that job when the tie rod broke on the truck he was driving. He tried to jump clear before the truck went into a deep ditch.

During the war years Homer began to grow some. Life even seemed eas-ier here because there was no rationing on gas or food.

Harris fished salmon in the Kodiak area with Virgo Anderson and Sam Pratt the seasons of 1944-1945.

After the Germans surrendered in 1945, Thelma took the children back to Minnesota to visit her family for the summer. While there that summer, the atom bomb was dropped, which brought about a quick surrender of the Japanese. Harris flew out and joined the family after the fishing season. They bought a car and drove to California, where they spent the winter with Harris' parents in Fullerton.

June of 1946 brought the family back to Homer after being delayed by a boat strike. Thelma's mother and sister, Grace, came for a summer visit also. Harris had come home earlier and fished that summer with his friend and neighbor, Hugh Watson. Harris' parents visited the fall of 1948. The road to Anchorage was being started. Harris was on the Kenai Peninsula Public Utility Board and the Library Board, which took quite a bit of time. Electricity became a reality in 1950. The road to Anchorage was passable by 1951.

From 1951 through 1955, Harris was employed year around with the Alaska Road Commission in Kenai. Headquarters for the family was in Kenai. However, it was a rather transient situation, with the children's summer work and higher education taking place elsewhere.

In 1955 Harris and Thelma moved back to the home place in Homer as Harris could have full time, year around employment with the Road Commission there.

In September of 1958, Harris and Thelma bought the Heady Hotel and operated it for fifteen years. After selling the Hotel in 1973 to David and Eileen Becker they built their retirement home on part of the original homestead.

Harris and Thelma celebrated their 50th wedding anniversary June 8, 1981.

The couple's children, Joan Edens, Joyce Farnen (deceased 11/15/81) and Galen Gordon raised their children in Homer. Sherry Ithal's family grew up in Anchorage. Harris and Thelma have fourteen grandchildren and eight great-grandchildren. There are four generations now living in Alaska. June 1986 marked the family's fiftieth year of residency.

WOODMAN HISTORY

(Contributed by Sanja Woodman Corazza)

In the summer of 1937 Oscar Woodman, his wife Mamie, their 18 yr. old son, Stan, and 16 yr. old daughter, Alice, along with their dog, Shep, left Ponsford, Minnesota in their 1936 V8 Ford sedan and began their journey to Alaska to become homesteaders. The journey took them a full year to make, as they worked their way northward.

In Seattle, the family rented a cabin on Aurora Avenue and they all found work in the area, picking apples, cutting cedar shakes, baby-sitting and other odd jobs. Over the winter Oscar secured a job as a stockman for Libby's cannery, located on the Kenai River in Alaska, and since this was the chance they had been waiting for, they sold the car and began final preparations for their move north. Oscar left early in the spring of 1938 by boat for Alaska and Mamie journeyed back to Minnesota to complete packing their belongings for the homestead life that lay ahead of them. In a rather interesting turn of events, Mamie, bereft of a car since they had sold the Ford, rode in a side-car beside her nephew Vernon's motorcycle with their dog Shep on her lap and it took five days of riding in that open side car to reach Minnesota. Once she had their belongings packed up she took the train back to Seattle, which gives some indication of how precious money was to the family and how carefully they were saving their dollars to prepare for life in Alaska.

In late August, Mamie, Stan, Alice and Shep took the Libby steamer David

W. Branch to meet Oscar. The trip took a week, with a welcome stopover in Yakutat, which gave some relief to the seasickness they were all feeling. Once in Kenai, they spent a week living in a tent waiting for a local tender to take them to Homer, an eleven-hour trip. Finally the Flyer, a salmon tender, took them, their supplies and newly acquired cook stove to the end of the Homer Spit, where there was no dock, so they all went ashore in skiffs. It was an exciting moment for the Woodman family; for all but Oscar, who had checked it out ahead of time, it was a first look at the area that would be their home for the remainder of their lives.

It was September and there were only two months left until the first snow normally fell, so along with new friends and neighbors they carted their belongings to the top of East Hill by hiking up the hill. At that time there was no road to the top of the hill and Stan remembers carrying load after load of flour up the trails that led to the homestead. They set up a tent near a spring on their land, and that spring was a blessing to them for good clear water in the Homer area was not easy to find, the majority of the water being laced heavily with iron that stained clothes and sometimes was undrinkable. The land had both natural meadows and thick forests so there were good trees for log cabin building and on November 1, 1938 they moved into their 14 -1/2' x 20' self-built log home. They were very grateful for the warmth from the new cook stove, because first that night it snowed and the next day there was a rolling earthquake, which surprised everyone. It was the beginning of an exciting but difficult first winter in Alaska.

Stan shot his first bull moose and the family was supplied with meat for the winter, but that first snow was the beginning of eight feet that would fall before spring finally arrived. As Stan and Alice said, "It was eight feet on the flat, not measuring the drifts!" The pictures taken that winter show Stan skiing above the roof of the cabin, and he enjoyed the novelty of skiing off the roof right onto the snow.

To make life even more difficult, Mamie became very ill, to the point that her life was in danger; it seems to have been a severe appendicitis attack, which took her many months to fully recover from. The Woodmans would find that their new home offered them clear water, meat for the taking, good ground for potatoes, strawberries, cabbages, carrots, and sugar beets, along with thoughtful homestead neighbors, but it also exacted a heavy toll. They fought heavy snows for six months out of the year, struggled to make a living in the Homer area, and found the men had to leave Homer for several months out of every year just to make wages; plus, they found they were far from their roots when it was twenty years before they saw their relatives in Minnesota again. Mamie, who had been one of a family of nine girls and two brothers, wrote long letters to her sisters, trying to keep family ties strong and tell them of the lives of her children and grandchildren.

In the spring, Stan snowshoed off the homestead to head for Kenai and his summer job. There wasn't a tender available at the time for transportation so a friend persuaded him that they could make the trip in his 16-ft. wooden skiff. They did make it to the Kenai River, but only because Stan bailed water with a bucket all the way! That was his last skiff ride from Homer to Kenai.

The second year on the land they built an addition on the cabin and also brought home from Libby's cannery a wonderful Guernsey milk cow, which they appropriately named "Libby". The cow needed a good barn, so the trees on the homestead were again put into use for shelter.

While Oscar did seasonal work for Libby's in Kenai and also began traveling north to Anchorage and Fairbanks to work for the Alaska Railroad as a special agent, Mamie made friends of the local homestead women and joined the Women's Club. She was a Christian and soon became part of the local group who started Christian Community Church in Homer. Along with several other homestead women, she helped organize Bible studies and taught many children in the area during Vacation Bible Schools.

The entire family learned to ski and spent many hours traveling over the hills to visit neighbors, or in Stan's case, skied as the only entertainment available. He and his friends, Erling Broderson, George Dahlgren, and Shorty Mauseth skied almost the entire Kenai Peninsula, hunting bear and moose and just exploring, one time skiing all the way to Seward, which was a grand adventure. In his later years it was hard to get him on skis because he said he had done his share of that kind of exercise! Once when Mamie wanted to go to see a friend but was lamenting because the snow was too deep, Stan tied a rope around her waist and then towed her on her skis to the neighbors. They built ski poles out of sticks and tin cans and made do with whatever equipment they had.

One year, just to prove that it's not always the men that get the moose, Stan and his friends skied off over the hills looking for the winter's meat, and while they were gone a moose walked by the cabin, so Mamie and Alice, with pounding hearts, shot it themselves. It was a great moment for them when the men came home empty handed to find a dead moose in the front yard. The ladies, no doubt, particularly enjoyed fixing dinners that winter.

Alice married Ben Bellamy and over the years they had seven children:

Don, Raymond, Marvin, Benny, Linda, Kenny and Judy. They spent part of those years on the homestead but found it difficult to support their children on homestead and local wages so in later years they moved around Alaska, from Portage to Glennallen to Anchorage, running businesses to support their family.

Stan began what would become a lifelong career in commercial fishing by starting off fishing with Fred and Virgo Anderson, seining from Homer all the way down the Alaska Peninsula with them, having adventures both on the boats and on land. He met many Native people on the Peninsula and developed friendships that lasted his lifetime. He thought highly of them and taught his children respect for the Native peoples of Alaska.

After only four years in Alaska, with an addition on the cabin, lovely gardens, hay meadows and a settled life, everything changed with the Japanese attack on Pearl Harbor. The men, Oscar, Stan and Ben, were called off to war and, during those years, the women were left alone on the hill. Alice remembered having to put black out curtains even on the windows of their little log cabin lighted only by kerosene lights, but she said they took it very seriously and they were often scared, especially when the Aleutians were attacked, and they honestly thought they would be next. Those were hard years for those left behind and for those who were in the Army.

Oscar led one of the first convoys over the Alaska Highway after it was completed and in his photo album are pictures of trucks full of supplies sinking through lakes and overturned on snowy hills.

Stan started off the war training out of Seward with the I Company of the 153rd infantry, and most of his company were soldiers from the Arkansas. It was a difficult experience for him because he became very good friends with all of those soldiers and, just as they were going to be shipped out to participate in D Day, he was pulled out of the company because he had been too many months without a furlough and legally they had to give him leave. His entire company was shipped to the beaches of Normandy and nearly every single man was killed; he was almost the only one left alive out of that group of men. For the rest of his life it was difficult for him to understand why he had been spared when all his friends died. Many of those men had married in Seward and so many women [were] left widows in that town.

Stan was later transferred into the Harborcraft division because of his boating experience, and in a ferocious winter storm with a skipper who he said, "was a fool because he followed the orders of a guy sitting at a desk with no windows and who didn't know boats," they shipwrecked on with no windows and who didn't know boats," they shipwrecked on Montague Island at MacCleod Harbor. The boat was the Q49 and it was so rough on the beach that the big Fairbanks-Morris engine was thrown through the side of the hull and they were only able to salvage a small amount of food. Stan organized a relay to save fuel and ammunition, weapons and 5 shovels and got into the one lifeboat that hadn't been destroyed. As they were making for the beach, trying to stay between the swamped boat and the beach for protection, a huge wave went right over the big boat, hit their lifeboat and "teakettled" it. They rolled over and over sideways in the freezing water but the big wave left them and the lifeboat high and dry on the beach when it retreated back to the ocean. The skipper had put out a distress call to Seward so the Army tried to rescue them after 3 weeks but while the rescuers were on shore another storm came up and left the 120 ft. barge in pieces just right for firewood, so they lived six weeks on the beaches of Montague Island, eating deer meat and digging clams. He said it was the best six weeks of the war for him! Stan also worked on the Portage Tunnel and is in the pictures of the first men through when it was finished.

After the war was over everyone tried to adjust to normal life again and Ben and Alice and their children moved into their own cabin on Alice's homestead, which was next to her parent's land. Mamie and Oscar tried their hand at different kinds of work to support themselves on their land ... chickens, haying, and other ideas, but Oscar kept having to return to railroad work to make a living.

Stan went back to his fishing career and eventually became one of the first gillnetters in Cook Inlet. Stan married Tonie Hawkes in 1950. She had come to Alaska as the first stop on her way around the world from Massachusetts, but instead of continuing her trip she married Stan and eventually they had two children, Sonja and Kim.

Today the Woodman homestead has three generations of Woodmans and Bellamys living on it and, surprisingly, some of the families continue to live, in part, as their grandparents did, enjoying the bounty of the land and going off fishing and running boats to make a living. The land still supplies clear water and the garden produces good potatoes, rhubarb and carrots. Moose still wander through the woods and the snow still reaches roof level some winters. Oscar and Mamie Woodman, who followed their hearts and dreams to Alaska, would surely enjoy seeing their great-great grandchildren playing in the grassy meadows on warm summer days and would know that the hardships they overcame planted a heritage for their generations.

NORTH TO THE FUTURE

(Story by William Edens)

My parents, Dick and Helen Edens, left Mississippi toward the end of the Great Depression for Sequim, Washington. There, three children were born: Dick Jr., myself, and sister Gwen. Dad had worked at a variety of things in order to keep bread on the table. Our next door neighbor was Garron Svedlund, who had a sawmill in Homer, where Rosi's shop now stands. He convinced Dad that living was much better in Alaska and that if he came to Homer, Dad could work with him in his sawmill cutting trap ties. After selling what he could, Dad packed up lock, stock (cow and chickens) and barrel (full of dishes).

We drove to Seattle, where we boarded the SS Yukon and sailed on April 22, 1939. The morning of the 29th was clear as we steamed into Kachemak Bay. Even at age six, I can remember the excitement of the beaches with all the shells, coal and driftwood. We arrived flat broke. Had dad had any money he would never have left the ship, the best break that could have come our way, I'm sure he would later admit. The steamship drained the gasoline out of the tank on the truck so he was unable to drive off the dock. The road to town was the old railroad bed. There was no gas station, so it was hard to find enough to get us to town. Had it not been for the kind-heartedness of Mae Harrington, who was the dock wharfinger and also happened to have a small cabin for us to live, and Lillian Walli, who owned Homer Cash Store and gave us credit on groceries, we would have been in a bad way. There was no work in town, even Garron, who had the mill, was not operating and fishing season was not for two months. The only lumber that Garron did saw was some for our homestead cabin that fall.

Dick and I finished school that spring with Mrs. Kohler as teacher. We learned more in those short three weeks than we had in the previous 8 months in Sequim. Dad went to Seldovia to work in the Seldovia Bay Cannery that summer. We raised a garden, cared for the cow and some goats that Ben Ridgeway brought up with us, carried coal off the beach and beach-combed glass balls. A Mr. Bennett stocked the old fox farm on Mae's property with blue foxes, which we helped to feed. This was the last of the commercial fox farms in Homer.

Before going to Seldovia, Dad had found 40 acres to homestead that Ernest Kirsch relinquished for us. That fall after returning home Dad built a 16 x 24 two-story cabin. This was to be our home for the next 5 years. The logs were taken from the 40 acres and were chinked with moss for the first two years then replaced with mortar. The interior had one large room for living and a small room large enough for a bed. Upstairs, where Dick and I slept, was gained by a set of stairs which more resembled an enclosed ladder due to its steepness. The cabin was heated with a wood/coal range, which had a large warming oven above. There also was a small tin wood stove for additional heat. We never had to worry about creosote build up nor do I ever remember having had a chimney fire. For the first two years we carried water from the spring. Mom had a large copper boiler in which we heated water for washing clothes and for bathing, which occurred in a large #3 tub. We ran to the outhouse. We moved into the cabin on the 18th of October with 8 inches of new snow on the ground. We kids were elated.

A log school was being built on the Pop Allen property about a mile away by the CCC's. Homer Heights School was completed just before Christmas and was celebrated with a big Christmas party. Gifts were given to all the kids. Homesteaders from all around the hill filled the one room. The school became the gathering place for church, games, and dance. School opened after the New Year with 12 students in grades 1-8. Margaret Richardson taught for three years. She lived in the teacher's quarters upstairs for two winters before she took up her own homestead. Water came from the adjacent creek, as well as the coal for heating. Homer Heights School boasted a twin two-holer with a storage area between.

Recess often lasted for more than 30 minutes since there were no fences and hard-to define boundaries. Many a lecture occurred as a result of our trifle extension of rules. The gullies and ridges made for excellent ski trails and was quick for getting away from the school but pleasingly difficult or slow coming back.

Dad made us our first pair of skis out of spruce lumber. He steamed the tips and held them in a clamp overnight. The binders were made out of belting. Those skis were our everyday transportation for the next four months. We kids had a lot of different ski runs. Several of the bachelor friends would come over and bomb out the trails. Our short skis turned shorter than the men's longer skis which bound and threw them off balance. Thus, so much for our trail until more snow fell. In the spring we kids made grass houses from alder frames covered with grass. We really had good times with little to do it with. We never ever thought that we were poor—no agencies to come around and inform us. We would have qualified for all kinds of aid by today's standards.

The third year, school was down to five students. This necessitated borrowing a student from under the hill since six were required. Darrel was to have been farmed around with several families but seemingly he spent the most time with us.

With the onslaught of W.W.II, many of the bachelors left, never to return. We covered our windows at night with some fear of the Japanese aggression. Since we had no food rationing, life seemed routine to us. Dick and I built trails down in the woods where we could watch the house and escape should the Japs come. It would have taken a rather blind soldier to miss us. Pop Allen was an interesting man in that he had an inventive way of entertaining himself. He would invite several bachelors over including the Bretts, who were of German decent. He would get the conversation going on the pros and cons of the war and then sit back and let the arguments fly, often to the point of being quite heated.

Summers found us putting up hay. We had Bob Cutler cut the wild grass for us once with his big white ox and drawn mower. Gene Kranich came over with a team of horses and cut for us another year while Dad was away fishing. We would put the hay up on shocks. This was accomplished by sticking an eight-foot pole into the ground and bracing with forked alder supports. The supports not only kept the shock upright but it kept the hay off of the ground. When dad came home in the fall, we would haul the hay into the barn. Spring came several weeks later up there since we were on the north slope of Bridge Creek. We kids would take the cow and calf over to the brow of the hill and let her graze for the day. We were over there the summer that the ARC put the road on past our place. We were quite interested in the equipment and would talk to the road crew, which was comprised mainly of Harris Gordon and Bob Kranich. As we looked down on the airport and Hater's Lake, now known as Nelsen Lake, and on some maps as Lampert Lake, they told us of the big whale that lived there and if we watched long enough we would probably see it. I don't recall ever seeing so much as a ripple on the lake, to indicate its presence. We were often found trying to repair the fence to keep the cow and calf in. We acquired an old dapple gray horse that had quite a personality. In winter when the snow was 3 to 4 feet deep, the trail to the watering hole became quite elevated. After the trail drifted shut, the horse would nip Beauty the cow on the rump until she would break the trail to the water. He would nudge her out of the way and break the ice, drink, allow her to drink and then repeat the process back to the barn.

Folks thought little of traveling some distance on foot to visit a friend or to help someone. Dad, Dick, and I hiked down town to a movie, which was being shown upstairs in Mrs. Walli's store. She had a light plant for electricity. After the movie, Dad got Bert Hansen to drive us up to the CCC Bridge in his Model A. I don't know how the conversation got started, but Bert proceeded to tell us of a little short fellow he knew who had to look through his steering wheel to drive. Of course, he had to give us a demonstration of this fellow and in the process ran off the road on the wrong side - if there was such a thing back then. We wound up having to hike most of the way home in the dark anyway.

I'll never forget my first job away from home. Bud Uminski came over to the house and asked if I could help him put up hay. I told him that Dick, Jr. was working over to Norman Ellis spud patch. "No, I want you" he repeated. I was elated and felt pretty big in that someone else wanted me. I was rewarded with our first kitten.

Dad put in a Bell sawmill, which helped to supplement our income. We took advantage of the sawdust pile and stored cakes of ice for ice cream during the summer. Mom made the best ice cream in Homer, using real cream from our Jersey/Guernsey cow. Erling Brodersen and George Dahlgren helped Dad in the mill. You could count on having ice cream most every night with them there.

My sixth and seventh grades were taught by Frances Heddell. She lived a good two miles or more from the school, which required walking or skiing each day. The roads were plowed usually twice a winter by the ARC cat. Once the plowed road drifted shut, it remained so till spring. Then came the mud and the frost boils which lasted through June. Gravel for the roads under the hill came from the gravel bar down by the slough, known now as Bishops Beach. The bar was at least 300 feet wide or more with driftwood piled high. There were lots of cedar logs to be found. A gravel bunker was built, by which a dump truck could back under a chute and then a cat would doze gravel in the hopper, filling the truck. Much of the gravel came from there for local construction until the airport was built. Gravel for it came from a large grassed bar out from Munson Point. In succeeding years gravel came from farther out on the spit around what was then green timbers. It finally came to the place that it was replenishing itself. In 1939, roads were graveled up to Bidarki Creek, a sprinkling up west hill road to Waddells and east to Thurstons (by Charlie Smiths).

Lillian Walli's store was a community-gathering place. There was most always someone sitting around her big oil heater ready to chew the fat. She also served as the community switchboard for the two phone systems. If someone on the hill wanted to talk with someone out east they would call her and she would ring their number, and when they answered she flipped a switch and you were on, as well as many busy bodies who thought they needed to keep up on the latest. Once at Homer Heights Jackie Myhill wanted some fun so he said, "Listen to this". He rang his home number knowing his mom had gone to town. Holding out the receiver we could hear at least a dozen clicks of receivers being raised. He loudly said, "Hang up Grandma." There was a momentary silence and then "click". There was the story of the family who had their radio antenna attached to the phone line. They didn't have to get out of their chair or stop their doings to learn of what was happening. There were frustrations to the system as well. Not only was your conversation community knowledge but there were busybodies that monopolized the line as well. Once we needed to get someone to come up the hill and take Dad and his gear to town in order to catch the tide. These ladies could hear the clicking of the receiver but would not give in. They continued to talk of root maggots and neighbors. Finally, Dad had to ask them to hang up. It still took time for their spring to unwind. The telephone lines were strung on native spruce poles and green trees. The wire was mostly galvanized phone wire, but as in several cases barbed wire worked just fine.

We moved off the homestead in 1945, as brother Dick was going into high school. Dad stated that he would not walk up and down the hill every day and did not think the kids should either. He bought 10 acres from Jim Waddell on the east hill. Jim would have sold him 120 acres with a livable house for $3,200. But Dad figured he didn't need that much ground to raise a few spuds. By this time, Dad had purchased the fishing vessel Jungle

Queen from Tom Shelford. Dick and I became the first kids to crew a fishing boat. This created quite a commotion in the industry, and soon many kids came on to deck hand. Dad took our family to Port Dick, where we camped on the beach. We had a real good time and learned to work as a unit, sort of like a machine. We helped Dad build five fishing boats, the largest being the Arctic Queen. We used this boat for gill netting for kings, reds, and living quarters for the seining season, and for crabbing. As poorer seasons came along, we saw the need to diversify our fishing. We split up our family partnership, with Dad taking a new combination seiner and Dick and I keeping the Arctic Queen. The new boat fished the Kodiak area and the Queen fished Cook Inlet and the outer district. About this time, 1958, Dick and I purchased Terminal Oil Sales from Tom Shelford. This included one worn out Ford Tanker and about thirty customers.

December 31, 1957, I was married to Joan Gordon, whom I first met in September of 1939. Her parents had come to Homer in 1936. We raised our three daughters, who still live in Homer - Shelly Erickson, Loree Edens and Beth Tutt. Now our grandchildren are being raised here in Homer.

Now 30 years later, we are still involved in the oil business and are growing with the area. We are developing the first private enterprise in the Homer Harbor; a marina called "Homer Fuel Dock".

I have been involved with varied community activities besides the Christian Community Church. As a commissioner on the Port and Harbor Commission I find it rewarding in being able to have some influence in the growth of the port. I worked on the Parks and Recreation Council for a number of years, and was named citizen of the year in 1973. I am a charter member of Igloo 32 Pioneers of Alaska.

It is difficult to put into a few words what it has taken 50 years to do. Alaska has been good to us. I appreciate the land and the creatures that inhabit it. Have you ever wondered what may have become of your life had you not come to Alaska? I can't imagine any other way. I appreciate my father and mother forsaking all others, so to speak, and heading "North to a Future", not only for themselves but for me as well.

HISTORY OF ARLEEN AND BOB KRANICH IN ALASKA

(By Arleen Kranich)

Our history in Alaska began in 1927 at Great Falls, Montana when Bob accepted a job running a sheep ranch at Chernofski, on Unalaska Island. I followed him a year later, arriving in mid-summer of 1928. We were married in the church at Unalaska soon after.

After running the sheep ranch for 7 years we saw a newspaper from Seward that described Homer as the "Shangri-La of Alaska". At that time we decided to move along, checking out Homer on the way.

We arrived in Homer in 1935 and homesteaded about 3 miles back in the hills (near Triple H Lumber). Selecting a homestead site was quite a chore as there were no roads up on the hill. Even after selecting a site, then came the job of locating the survey markers in the 5 - 6 ft. tall grass.

We had livestock shipped in from Oregon that included 100 sheep, 4-5 cattle and 3 horses. Also included in that shipment was haying machinery, household furniture including an "inside" bathroom fixture, which may have been the first one in Homer. This shipment was unloaded at the end of the Spit from a scow, since there was no dock at the time. Later my father sent us 3 turkeys which were the beginning of our turkey flock which increased to about 100. We had success in increasing the herds, but due to poor communications, lack of transportation and the long winter feeding periods, it was not very profitable.

During the years on the homestead we were never lacking for something to do. Along with the usual stock tending and haying there were always extra undertakings. One of these projects involved Bob being hired as local director of the CCC, which built the roads up both East and West hills and built a dock on the end of the spit. Of course, in order to build a dock, the men had to go across the bay to McKeon Flats to fall trees that were skidded to the water and floated to the spit to be used for the dock piling.

Another venture that kept us busy was in the winter of '40-'41 when arrangements were made for us to provide school bus service, transporting the students to the "Hill School" over across Bridge Creek. When weather and road conditions permitted, our school bus was a Model A pickup that we built a wooden cab on back of to provide shelter for the kids. As alternate buses we used a horse drawn buggy or a sled that was towed by our Allis Chalmers gas cat.

Along with these many activities Bob and Turk Monroe found time to log and run a sawmill to cut lumber for us and supply lumber for many of the homesteads round about.

While we were homesteading we started our family. We had two fine sons. Bill was born Nov. 14, 1936 in Seward. Due to a bad fall I had, Ray was in a hurry and didn't wait the whole term. He was born without fingernails or cartilage in his ears and these were developed after birth. He was born in Anchorage weighing 4 pounds 5 ounces at midnight July 2, 1940. He was one of the last babies born in the old railroad hospital before it was closed and torn down.

In 1943 Lydia Shelford, Postmaster, had to go outside due to the illness of her husband, Tom. Lydia asked me to be Postmaster and I was officially installed in April of 1944. We sold our livestock and machinery and left the homestead ranch to move to town. We didn't realize that when Bob and his friend were sawing lumber they had also made the lumber for our home in downtown Homer, which would also be the Post Office until about 1953.

We entered into the mainstream of Homer life. It seemed we were "so handy" to spread information, etc. for everything that was happening. Bob was chosen as representative for the farmers to negotiate with the U.S. Navy in Kodiak for selling them produce from the local farms.

It was in connection with the farm produce that Bob went to Palmer to see how they packaged their produce to sell in Anchorage. While Bob was in Palmer he went into the office of REA (Rural Electric Association) to inquire about getting electricity for the Homer area. It took 5 years of paperwork and weekly meetings, but Bob never gave up on his dream to have Homer electrified. After Homer was energized, Bob turned his talents to other organizations and services in the community to help with other projects.

Several organizations came into fruition at this time in Homer's history, and because of our location at the Post Office and our willingness to help, we were involved in all of them. These included the Homer Civic League, CCC, HEA and the PUD which helped promote the dock, school, fire hall, hospital and the library, to name a few.

While getting settled into the town lifestyle, Bob went to work for the Alaska Road Commission, working on Homer's fledgling road system. For many years he was the main "cat skinner" and did the initial roadbed building and gravel spreading to build many of the areas early roads. In those days, of course, there were no paved roads and they didn't have any trucks or trailers large enough to carry a "cat", so if they needed it across town, Bob would walk it on the road, many times taking several hours getting to where the work was. It was said that, "he wore one D-6 out several times" just walking it back and forth across town.

Bob worked for the ARC until statehood, then joined the state highway department, working until around 1968 when he retired.

As I continued my job as Homer's Postmaster, the mail volume was ever increasing, especially the parcel post. The regular, or surface mail, as well as the parcel post, was shipped to Seward by steamer and then trucked to Homer and points in between twice a week by Walt Christensen. Homer had grocery service provided by Lilly Walli and the Berrys, but Sears Roebuck and "Monkey Wards" provided Homer's apparel.

Bob and I built the Family Theater in 1957 because of the boys' urging to have a pleasant place for family picture shows. Our first admission prices were 35 cents for kids, 50 cents students and 90 cents adults, a far cry from today! Our sons worked at the theater until they left home and then I graduated to projectionist. Bob and I continued to run the theater until 1970, at which time Bob decided to retire from that business also.

Since Bob was retiring, I did the same. Twenty-seven years and twenty days after my appointment as Homer's Postmaster, I retired. About this time, in celebration of our anniversary, Bob presented me with a gold Cadillac—Homer's first. It was pretty big for parking and used a lot of gas, so it was eventually traded in for a motor home. Having the motor home to travel with, Bob and I wintered in Florida and then spent summers in Homer from 1971 until 1978 when he became ill; passing away in the fall of 1979.

One of my most memorable moments was on the homestead in the late summer of 1936. We were haying the last meadow, which would make the last outside stack, since we were building a large hay barn. I was seven months pregnant and had gained in size and weight. I took a look at the meadow and made a base for a last stack. When Bob came in he said it was too large and made a smaller base. As they brought in load after load of hay, the stack got higher and higher. I thought, "how will I ever get down?"

I tried to tell Bob my worry, but he said, "we'll get you down." Then the "cleanup" load was added to my stack. At the finish I was at least 30 feet in the air. To get me down Bob put a 10-ft. ladder against the stack and Turk Monroe, who was the taller, stood on top of the ladder and reached up. He had to stick two haying forks into the stack, tines curved up to stabilize them, so I would have two steps. I had to come down forward because of my big belly. Balancing myself with my fork, I carefully slid down to where Turk could catch my feet and guide me down to the ladder he then helped me down to the ground where Bob was waiting.

Memories like these I would never trade. I am proud that my husband, Bob, and I are a part of Alaska and Homer history. It was and is a good life!

A TRIBUTE TO BOB AND ARLEEN KRANICH

(By their Sons Ray & Bill)

We are pleased to have this opportunity leave a monument of sorts, to our parents, Bob and Arleen Kranich. In addition to being the loving, caring parents of us boys, they were "pillars" in their community - the memory of which should not be forgotten.

Dad (1904-1979) gave us a fine example of wisdom, hard work and persistence, while being of selfless service to the community to such areas as Homer Civic League, Homer Electric Association, Public Utility District #1 and Homer City Council to name a few. He was never too busy, however, to help us with our problems or to put a humorous "twist" on them so they were easier to bear. He was a good guy to have on your side.

Mom (1902-present), despite her full-time job as Postmaster, plus other civic activities, was always there to support Dad (and us) in whatever endeavor we were involved. From boosting Boy Scouts to providing refreshments for the Homer Electric Association organizational meetings, to "care packages" to sons away from home, she could always be counted on. Her "extra-curricular" activities over the years included Homer Woman's Club, Library Board, American Cancer Society, as well as others. We appreciate her tireless example of good-hearted helpfulness, and her fine example of how not to take one's self too seriously.

It would be a big order to fill their shoes, but we are grateful for the tracks they left for us to follow.

THE FIRST FISH PLANT

First there was the Jones' little cannery located where Land's End Hotel is today (Earl Hillstrand would buy the property from the Jones' when the highway was pushed through from Anchorage).

Eight members of the Jones family came from Vaughn, Washington, in 1939 to establish a seafood cannery, "Homer Spit Packing Company". They came on the Alaska Steamship Lakina. Alfred Jones was the member who knew exactly what to do. He built a small cannery building lined with metal to be easily washed down. For power, they had a steam boiler and a separate small gas engine to pump salt water from the Bay for cleansing. Fresh water for their 700-gallon tank was hauled to the Spit by Shorty Price, with his wagon and team of horses.

They had a twenty-foot skiff which they rowed to get fish: pink salmon and clams from China Poot Bay, Dungeness crab from pots set out around the east side of the Spit, as well as red salmon from set nets. To imagine rowing a twenty-foot skiff across the Bay to China Poot, fishing and digging clams, then rowing back, loaded and heavy, regardless of the weather, because the pack had to be canned while the fish were there, seems more than the human body could endure.

Paul Jones, age 13, was assigned the job of cleaning the salmon, and his meticulous Uncle saw that they were spotlessly clean. Shucking the crab was the biggest job in the canning process, but even so, they would can five cases of half-pound flats a day of crab. Proof of the quality of their pack was that it was purchased by the famous buyer Ivar Wendt, who paid the going price when he took the pack, and then at Christmas, sent a bonus check.

The cannery lasted ten years with some additions of the Jones family, like Freda Cole, who also worked in the cannery, as well as Homer ladies like Hazel Heath, Minnie Harrington and Vera Schoate. Paul Jones now speaks of it as no big deal; what I call a real pioneer!

D. T.

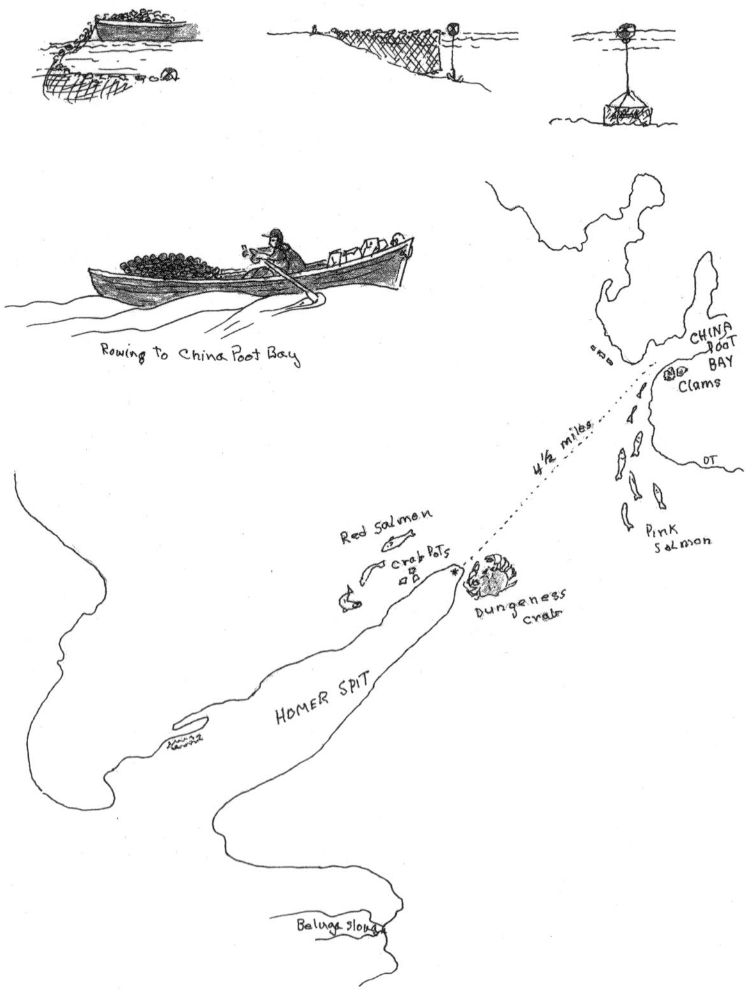

TEPA HANSON ROGERS AND SHIRLEY SHOLIN'S STORY - 1954

I include this history of Homer written by Tepa Hanson Rogers and Shirley Sholin in 1954. Both girls were born in Homer, as their family narratives relate. It repeats many stories written by others, but adds another perspective, giving a broadened view of the times, and dramatically demonstrates the positive energy that made it all possible.

Diana Tillion

Along the north and the east shores of Kachemak Bay, as far southeast as Seldovia, north to the Susitna River and as far west as the valley of the Kuskokwim, once dwelt a mighty and a proud branch of Athabaskans, the Tanaina. Their domain embraced all of the Cook Inlet area and far more. If one wishes to read about these original inhabitants of the Homer area he should read Osgood's Ethnography of the Tanaina, published by the Yale University Press. However, this present paper does not include these romantic peoples, nor the vast area they inhabited, but it does include a particle of their domain. Just as these cultures lived from the abundance of Kachemak Bay and Cook Inlet and the fertile soil adjoining them, so do the present inhabitants of Homer and vicinity.

Homer has been likened to Shangri La. There is no specific place of beginning or ending. Homer stretches from the hills along side the Bay and the Inlet, even meandering on top of the hills, as well as out to the end of the Spit. Homer has no responsible civic authority beyond the limited authority relegated to its Public Utility District Board of Directors. As yet, even

Homer's residents are unable to tell a newcomer where the town is (or even if it is).

There is irrefutable evidence that this area was visited by Russian trappers and explorers during the latter part of the eighteenth century. They raised vegetables successfully in several places along the Bay and Inlet. Not too long afterwards, the famed British explorer, Captain Cook, visited the same area. Whereas the Russians sought furs and geographic data, Cook sought the ever-elusive Northwest Passage.

In 1849, Tevenkof first entered the Bay where the present town of Seldovia is now situated. Also, he established a trading post on Yukon Island. From these posts, the Russians obtained many furs, and in particular sea otter. Several cabins were built at Halibut Cove and, supposedly, one or two erected along the Homer Spit.

Shortly after the United States purchased Alaska, the American government sent an expedition to survey the Peninsula. A military post was established where the old Russian post stood at Kenai. The explorers reported to the government in Washington that the country was ideal pastureland.

The first permanent settlement (other than native) was made, however, by the Russians on the Kenai Peninsula at Kasilof in 1786, three years before George Washington was inaugurated President. They mined the local coal beds which were discovered by Portlock.

In the 1890's an English Company opened a coal mine at Bluff Point near where Homer was to be born. For a number of years this mine was operated successfully. Later a standard gauge railroad was built from the coal mine to the Spit. Mrs. Lillian Walli remembers that when she first came to Homer in 1914 the rails were still intact and that a handcar was still used by the local citizenry. The railroad ran along the beach and caused the original Beluga Lake. A roundhouse was built at the end of the Spit and the railroad was operated until the coal mine was closed down in 1907 by an Act of Congress withdrawing from entry all the coalfields. There was a half-moon dock at the Spit where regular steamers pulled in to receive their loads of coal and passengers who were bound for the gold fields of Hope and Sunrise. Many of these people were picked up by the steam schooner, L. J. Perry, which was partly owned by the famous Alaskan, "Cap" Lathrop, who became Alaska's most famous capitalist and benefactor. "Cap" was a frequent visitor to the town, as he plied the Inlet carrying passengers and freight, as well as the latest "Stateside" news.

It was early in the Spring of 1896 when Homer was born and established on the end of the Spit. The Alaska Gold Mining Company, headed by a Michigan man by the name of Homer Pennock, brought a crew of some fifty men on the schooner Excelsior to the end of the Spit in Kachemak Bay, just about 100 years after the Russians established the first peninsula colony at Kasilof. At this time the Alaska Gold Company was interested in prospecting the area. Homer Pennock, the namesake of Homer, was manager and promoter of this enterprise. The original party consisted of approximately 75 persons, one of who was the pioneer woman, Della Murray Banks. Years later, while reminiscing, Mrs. Banks took great pride in calling herself "the Original Inhabitant". When this party first landed all they found was an old abandoned cabin built from the remains of some ill-fated galley which had gone aground.

During this time, two other mining ventures began and the town of Homer on the Spit grew so rapidly that it soon had several hundred inhabitants, a post office, warehouse, and many other buildings. The first of these companies was the Kachemak Coal Field Company, which died when the Matanuska Coal Fields were opened by the Alaska Railroad. The other venture was known as the Homer Coal Mine and was organized by John Herbert. He shipped coal to Hope, Sunrise, and to Anchorage via barges pulled by the S.S. Bidarky and the S.S. Titonic. Some of his coal was also consumed by the local canneries that had sprung up. However, this company closed shop in 1924. In the meantime the Town of Homer on the Spit was destroyed by fire during a savage storm, the town being completely devoid of any sort of fire protection equipment. From the original Spit site the residents just pulled off onto the beaches below Homer Hills, where Homer now begins and ends. Fresh water was a problem for these early settlers on the Spit after the ice melted. They took barrels and went by sailboat across the bay to a waterfall and once with a lighter to the bluff at the foot of the Spit. Either procedure was always a difficult daylong affair and a struggle against the wind and tide.

Much progress has been made in the agricultural development of the Homer area since its first farms began in 1915. Mr. Charles Miller, for whom Miller's Landing is named, first came to Homer as an employee of the Alaska Railroad. They employed him to winter 95 horses on the abundant native grasses around Homer. Mr. Miller began to farm and successfully so until he retired in 1953. For a while he also operated a fox farm. He tells of going by rowboat to Seldovia for his supplies.

Whereas today many farms are beginning to pay their own way and to make a creditable living for their owners, it was not always so. From 1915 until 1936 few managed to make much of a living on farms hereabouts. At the latter time many settlers began to move on Homer as homesteaders. Several ranches were established, but again, due to the lack of markets, poor communications and transportation difficulties, the ventures failed.

Around 1914, Andrew and Ed Sholin began fox farming in the local area. Mr. Walli went with the Sholins by skiff and foot to Sheep Mountain and dug out foxes to get their start. This type of farming caught the fancy of people like wildfire. For a short time there were at least fifteen such farms, in addition to several mink farms. However, fur farming, too, was short lived for perhaps three allied reasons: the lack of sufficient food (moose and porcupines), excessive cost of production, and the fall in fur prices. The Kenai Peninsula was once one of the great trapping regions of Alaska.

One of Homer's most profitable and long-lived industries began in 1920. At that time fishing boats were put into the Bay and Inlet. These original boats were owned by local canneries. There were once as many as ten fish traps between Homer Spit and Stariski Creek. Ten years later, the first privately owned vessels began to ply local waters. Since this time, private vessels have taken a big part of the fish products in the area. At one time herring were so plentiful that fishermen reaped tremendous profits from their sale, and Halibut Cove was a thriving town. Due, though, to overfishing and lack of conservation practices, the herring disappeared around 1926. Only recently have faint evidences of their return been noticed. Today, local fishermen haul in quantities of salmon, crabs, clams, shrimp, and halibut.

Out of this fishing industry has grown a constant demand for local boat building and docking facilities. Boat building has never been pushed very far though. The first definite and concrete work on dock facilities was begun in 1938 by the Homer Civic League. Up until that time freight was landed on the beach below Chamberlain's Store and everyone went down and picked out their own stuff. The Civic League under Sam Pratt's leadership constructed the first dock for modern Homer. It was 180 feet long with a 60-foot face. The League sawed its own lumber and with, some CCC help, put up the dock. The receivers of any freight did their own longshoring. The present dock was constructed by the Alaska Road Commission back in 1949, while Claude Rogers was general foreman of the Road Commission here. This same Civic League built the road across the foot of Beluga Lake, giving Homer an all weather road to the Spit.

The general influx of inhabitants necessitated a more adequate means of communication and transportation into the area. The very first road built in Homer was constructed in 1925, beginning at Miller's Landing and stretching two miles in either direction. This meager beginning was supplemented in 1926 by road building westward to the west schoolhouse, which stood west of the present school and neared the bluff. In 1927, crews carried the road eastward to about where Emma and George Miller now live, and the same year a road was built to the Slough and the Spit. Preceding this time, those wishing to go to the Spit [had] to wait upon Father Neptune and the tides. This old crossing was via the beach where the gravel pits are at the lower part of town. Today, roads connect Homer with Seward, Anchorage, Interior Alaska and the States, but only since 1950. In addition to this arterial connection there are approximately 35 miles of local roads serving the needs of the rural population. Almost yearly these roads are pushed farther into the woods and new homes are built on the extensions.

Another need for the sprawling community was a means of communication. From 1923 to 1946 an old-fashioned, country-style, telephone system, with its lines strung on tripods, mushroomed from Fritz Creek to Schaffers and onto the end of the Spit, and even up on top of the hill into the back country, serving the scattered homesteaders. Every fall, men of the community turned out and worked on the poles, lines, etc. If any consumer failed to pay his share of the cost he was immediately cut off. This happened only one time, however. In 1934, Sam Pratt started a second communication service under the Alaska Communication System. The call letters were KEAI. This venture proved economically unsatisfactory and was allowed to lapse in 1936. Then in 1946, the Arctic Telephone and Telegraph System was established. It grew into the present Homer Radio Station. The present means of communication, the Homer Telephone Company, is comparatively new, having been installed in 1951 by Homer and Mary High.

Although Homer's first post office was on the Spit—as mentioned elsewhere in this paper—another was begun in modern Homer in 1921 with Mrs. Henry Wells as first Postmaster. Since that time, two buildings near where Grandma Burns now lives served as a post office. For a number of years Mr. and Mrs. Shelford were Postmasters. Mrs. Shelford moved the post office into one room of their home, where it remained for years. Later, Mrs. Kranich became Postmaster. The post office remained in Mrs. Shelford's home, but eventually Mrs. Kranich moved it into one room of her home and later in 1952 into its present building.

Homer's first school was opened back in 1919 on the old Neilson Ranch, beyond Miller's Landing. It was soon moved into the community hall on the same ranch. Mrs. Nellie McCullough was the first teacher. The second teacher was Mrs. Flindahl, during whose term the school burned down. The occasion was a Christmas celebration, the cause an overheated stove. The school was rebuilt at Miller's Landing and is now Boyd's Grocery warehouse. In 1924, the West-end school was established in a cabin on the Harrington land near the bluff and west of the present school buildings, with Mrs. Flindahl as teacher. Shortly before the fall term began, Homer residents built a new school, which is now incorporated in the Benson residence. In these two original West-end schools there had only been six pupils—of which two were boarding students brought over from Seldovia in order to have sufficient numbers to merit a school. Since that time, our school has rapidly expanded in enrollment and in facilities. In 1942 the old wing of the present building was built. This served until 1952, at which time the new concrete addition was added. Just as the school population has overgrown all other buildings in the past, so has it now outgrown the present facilities. From the enrollment of six, it has grown to over two hundred; from one teacher to a staff of nine. Even now, hopes exist that new additions will be made, new teachers added and the school curriculum expanded to include a completely equipped high school.

To provide social outlets the original inhabitants began the organization of various clubs, the first of which was the Woman's Club, organized in 1934. The meeting place of this original club was the building presently used as the Homer Bakery. This building has served in numerous other capacities including that of a community center. Today there are clubs for every social activity one might want in Homer. To be exact there are close to forty local clubs and organizations.

One of the most intensely felt needs of the citizenry was spiritual. Even before the erection of definite places of worship, many worship evenings were spent by the spiritually minded in various homes, singing hymns lustily, and in prayer meetings. It was inevitable that so long as such longings lay in their hearts the residents would soon gather into small groups and organize religious institutions. Perhaps one of the earliest movements was that for a community church without creed or denominational affiliation. Thus it was that in 1940 the first such church was organized, with Carl Taylor as pastor. Shortly afterward, Lee Byers followed Rev. Taylor and remained in Homer until the present Community church was completed in 1948.

The Adventist church was begun around 1944 and was used for only a short while. Myrle Smith was pastor. At present their services are held in private homes.

Perhaps Paul Marteeny conducted services in his home on the hill. When members started moving off the hill he bought a lot on which the church now stands. With money received from a group of California Churches he bought a sawmill and cut timbers from his homestead to begin the Church. Rev. Johnston was secured as pastor in 1947. For one summer Rev. and Mrs. Gates served as pastors. Since then they have established the Alaskan Christian Home out on the East Road where orphan children are taken care of and given schooling. The Home has been given top rating by the Territory among institutions of its kind.

The Homer Methodist Church is three years old. Its pastor was Cecil Wyant. The first services were held in the American Legion Hall. At present it meets in the Quonset Hut on Main Street; Rev. Nelson Moyer pastor. This church owns its own pastorage and plans a church building in the near future.

Rev. Dale Davis came to Homer as pastor of the Community Church, but left shortly afterwards to organize the Homer Baptist Church in 1952. It now meets in the Husky Building.

In 1947, Mrs. Lenferink donated 1/2 acre for a Catholic Church. It was decided that the time was not right for a building program, so Mass had been held in the theater once monthly. Later it was held at the Inlet Inn and now is held in a building donated by Jack Mills and is known as the Church of St. John. Father Arnold Custer of Seward drives to Homer every third Tuesday to hold two-day services.

In November 1953, the local Episcopalian group was organized and holds services in private homes. Russell Clapp, the rector at Mathias [was brought] by Rt. Rev. Bishop Gordon, the flying Bishop of Alaska on his visit to Homer in February of 1954. At that time two children were baptized and one adult confirmed.

Very early the residents of our town began to investigate the possibility of having community electrification. During the fall of 1945, a public meeting was held to investigate such possibilities. This was the meeting that finally got action and Rural Electrification Authorities were contacted and definite plans were launched. Finally, in 1947, a loan of more than $200,000 was approved, and, in 1950, another loan in excess of $350,000 was made. Homer Electric Association became a reality and nearly all the homes in Homer are connected with the system. The lines run up on top the hill and out beyond 6 mile, with plans to run very soon as far as Clam Gulch.

No town can become attractive to settlers, mature and sufficient unless it has varied business establishments. The first such institution was operated by Anton Johanson, who brought his supplies in from Seldovia. His store was down by the slough where the old Spit road crossed. This was about in 1919. Then in 1923, the venerable Henry Olsen had a store on the Munson Ranch. He imported his supplies from "Squeaky" Anderson of Seldovia. Henry would open up only when someone wanted something; otherwise he went on tending his cattle on the West slope. Bert Hanson had one of those little-bit-of-everything stores in a shed behind his house. His supplies came from Chambers in Seldovia. Bert was bought out by Walli's in 1936.

Though the first store has disappeared, as did the first coal mine, the first gold mining operation, the first town site and many of the first farms; many other businesses have sprung up that now serve practically every need of the local residents. There are restaurants, general merchandise stores, a meat market, a bakery, bars, a cold storage plant, gasoline and service stations, inns, hotels, tourist courts, gasoline storage tanks, realtors, hardware stores, lumber mills and suppliers, an insurance agency and other suppliers of needs—material and otherwise. There are longshoremen, carpenters, fishermen, farmers, churchmen, school teachers, all working with and for the greatest resource of all people, themselves, making a community where people like to live.

In addition there are other institutions that render needed services: The CAA, Homer Telephone Exchange, Homer Radio Station, the Bank of Homer and the Local Air Strip. Incidentally, this strip was completed in 1941 and the bank was organized in 1950 by Arthur Hewlett. The present Homer Radio Station began full operation in 1952 and yet the end isn't in sight. The present Citizens Study Group emphasizes repeatedly the need for year round industry to furnish steady employment. The resources are available and the population is ready to come here. Homer's progress is as sure as is that of any self-propelling industrious group of citizens.

Local order and government have been felt needs. Attempts have been repeatedly made to secure some form of local government. In 1949, a Public Utility District became Homer's form of government. Since that time, attempts have been made to incorporate either as a school district or as a town. All such attempts have so far failed, and the PUD remains the only civil authority. The Marshal from Kenai or a Highway Patrolman is called in when any serious trouble befalls Homer. There is a local US Commissioner, however, for minor disturbances and to keep the district records.

Currently the citizens Study Group (brought to Homer by Mr. Wm. L. Mathews of the Bank of Homer and a goodly group of forward-looking citizens) is the most spontaneous demonstration of popular self criticism ever demonstrated by any community in Alaska. It is attempting to analyze the community and to provide a basis whereby Homerites might unite to make their town all that they hope it to be. Through it, citizens are examining every institution of the town critically, not from a destructive standpoint, but constructively, with the ultimate purpose of devising activity groups, which will do the job of opening up new opportunities and fostering more progress. The first such activity group to be activated is the Beautification Committee, which will hold Homer's Modern Clean-up Day on May 16, 1954. Following the lead of this committee, others are formulating plans of a similar nature.

Thus we see Homer in 1954— and now it has sprung from hardships and adversities. Homer has had a series of rises and falls—or as the historian, J. B. Caldwell would say, it has grown because of its hardships and the will of its people to overcome those adversities.

1. Even previous to the Athabaskan culture there was an occupation in prehistoric times by Eskimos. In fact, the Kachemak Bay and Cook Inlet regions are very rich in old village sites where over 4700 artifacts have been found. Reference: See Frederica De Lagun's book, <u>The Archaeology of Cook Inlet</u>, Alaska, in the Homer Public Library.

2. Merle Colby, in his book, <u>A Guide to Alaska, Last American Frontier</u>, published in 1944, says of Homer, "...its population (35) as listed by the census of 1930 gives no hint of its growing importance. By 1937, 150 farmers had arrived in this fertile area, and many more applications were on file ... Almost unbelievable stories of bumper crops find their backing in the sober records of farmers in the settlement....One Seattle produce house has a standing offer for Homer turnips at a premium of a cent a pound higher than Seattle prices." That in 1944.

3. The members of that first Homer Civic League still living in Homer are: Mrs. Lillian Walli, Sam Pratt, The Anderson Boys, Tom Shelford, Carl Sholin, Jack Deitz, Carl Baiers, Charlie Miller, The Neilson Boys, Guy Waddell, Al Kranich, Mr. Bowers and Mr. Nordby.

Grateful acknowledgment is given to all those who helped compile this history, and in particular to Mr. S. S. Gnad and Alsa F. Gavin, who put memories of Homer's many old timers into words.

BANK   OF   HOMER, Inc.,

Homer, Alaska

Dear Subscriber :-

It gives me great pleasure to inform you that our total capital of $ 15,000. has now been subscribed, and a list of the subscribers is enclosed for your information.

The next step is to get the subscriptions paid in, hold our first stockholders meeting for the election of Directors and apply to the Territorial Banking Board for permission to engage in a banking business. I hope very much to be able to accomplish this by January 2.

If you will please forward me your check drawn to the order of the Bank of Homer, Inc., a receipt will be issued pending authority to issue your shares of Capital Stock. Your check will be deposited in the First National Bank of Anchorage until such time as we are permitted to open the bank for business.

Many thanks for your subscription and your support of this project.

Sincerely yours,

ARTHUR T. HEWLETT

October 27, 1949

Arthur and Natalie Hewlett

THE BANK OF HOMER, RECALLED BY NATALIE HEWLETT

When my husband, Arthur, and daughter, Anna, and I flew down to Homer there were eighteen hundred people and no road. Arthur decided Homer needed a bank. He wrote to a fraternity brother who was a banker, to ask if he would invest in a bank in Homer. He wrote back he would be glad to invest, but you had to involve the people of Homer to invest in the bank. We made a list and went to interview people, and to our astonishment they had money in tin cans under their beds. No one refused, but one merchant.

We divided our basement in our house, making two teller windows and a small counter for customers to write deposit slips. Then, we needed a safe. On route to Alaska, on Alaska Steam Ship, I met Elsie Stouffer, principal of schools in Ketchikan. She would soon be going to Egigik, Alaska to work in a cannery for the summer; returning she would look for a safe in Seattle. She found two little safes. Remember, in those days freight came by measurement, not weight. We had a terrible time getting those safes to the basement. Eventually, we built a vault under our front steps of our house, and had a time lock door installed.

Arthur hired Tepa Hansen to help him. She proved to be a devoted employee and Arthur had great respect for her. He also hired a local gentleman. They operated the bank for a little over a year, then on a Saturday at

2:00 am, this gentleman had a coronary thrombosis. There was no doctor in Homer and I was afraid to give him anything. Then, he had another attack, which ended his life. I called my friend, Helen Alm, and she came down. As soon as the news was out, the FDIC inspector came and said that the body had to be sent to Anchorage, for an autopsy.

They found a discrepancy in the bank's accounts. That gentleman had signed savings accounts and taken the money to finance his motel. I thought there would be a run on the bank, so I sent to Anchorage for all the one dollar bills I could get so I could pay out the money slowly. There was no run on the bank, which was a great compliment to Arthur.

Then I hired Electa Bolton to work in the bank. The first customer, Ethel Scott, owner of a grocery store, came upstairs to tell me if Electa worked in the bank she would withdraw her account. It was a problem; I had only just hired her, it was only her first day. So I went down and said to Electa that I was just sitting around with nothing to do and I would like to work in the bank. I sure wished I had worked in the bank when Arthur was alive.

After two years, I decided to sell the bank and Elmer Rasmuson, of NBA, was the most businesslike of all the offers. Now there is a big new building for the bank and a road into Homer. And, as Arthur predicted, Homer grew and grew.

In addition to the Bank and HEA coming to Homer, making a dramatic change, the other three most substantive endeavors were Earl Hillstrand's Land's End Hotel; Icicle Seafoods, that brought more fish folks to homer, and, subsequently, Ken and Snooks Moore's Northern Enterprise boat yard, providing critically needed supplies and repairs for the burgeoning fleet. Each of these businesses took the gamble and the tenacity of the true Pioneer Spirit.

On a personal level, three nurses lived in Homer. Wilma Cowgill, who was a pioneer and provided medical advice and assistance when needed, was joined by Helen Alm and Natalie Hewlett in times of crisis. These ladies were the mainstay of immediate health care, to either take care of the situation or get the patient off to Anchorage or Seldovia to a doctor. After Homer had a resident doctor, it was not forgotten what a wonderful trio they were, and their portrait hangs in the Homer Hospital today.

D. T.

Special thanks go to those Pioneer family members that shared their recall:

To Ray and Bill Kranich, who delved into their family archives to find the Minutes of the Civic League and other information.

To Bill Wakeland, who shared his photos. Unfortunately, this book includes only the Pioneer Period, so we couldn't use all the incredible photos that he has on file. Many of those can be seen at Land's End.

To Steve Thurman of Halibut Cove, who owned and repaired Steve Zowistowski's boat, the Normandy, which was one of the small boats used to haul the mail and passengers from Seldovia, before donating it to the Pratt. The boat is an all too clear reminder what it was like when that was the only type of transportation.

The photos only touch a few of the Pioneers who made Homer happen. The names in the Civic League add those who took part in the organization of the town and its needs. There were many others who aren't named here simply because that information wasn't available.

This is a tribute to those in these pages and those who are not. They were, indeed, and industrious group!

PHOTOS

FROM THEIR ALBUMS
JUST A FEW OF THISE HANDSOME PIONEERS

Bert Hansen. Alfred Anderson. Phinna Bowers. Charley Miller.
Carl & Ann Sholin. Bob & Alrlene Kranich. Homer Latham.

This is a photo of Charley with a group of horses on the grass plain that was Homer Spit. The Dept. of Agriculture's agent reported that there was much good pasture land near Homer. Please note in that this photo of the horses shows a set of telegraph (or phone) poles running along the East side of the Spit. Using a square and assuming where that location of Green Timber Slough used to be what the following map shows is that where the camera stood was at least a mile and a half further west than the present edge of the Spit.

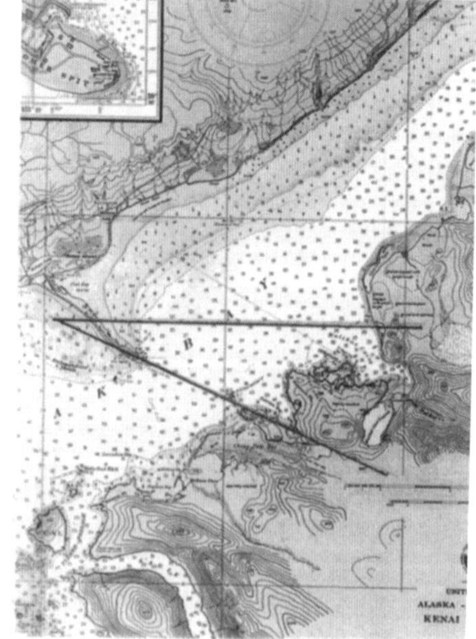

Samuel Nielsen with son's William and Starr came in 1914 from Denmark.

Samuel's wife Martha with baby Stanley. Early 20's.

Son Karl Nielsen tends the horses during haying while an unrecognizable man works the top of the stack.

Nielsen's new automobile.

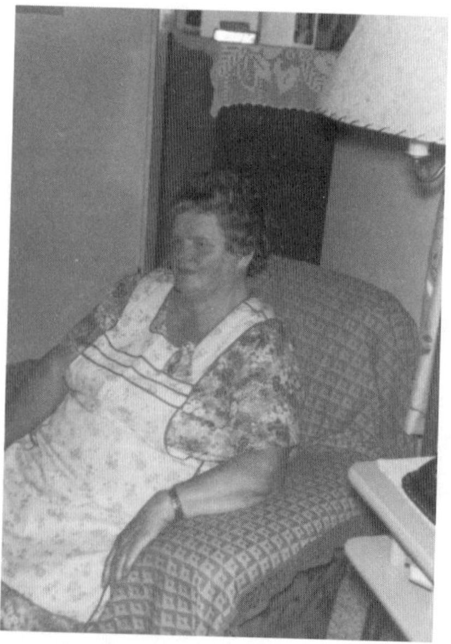

Ma Walli rest for just a moment.

Then to the Laundry.

Young Lillian and Benny Bowers.

Ronnie Mars, Lillian Walli and Milo Kallman.

Karl Rosenburg

Ero, baby Robert, and Lillian Walli.

Miss Lillian the cowgirl.

At Laura Frazier's Homer Women's Club Meeting: Mary Price (seated) Alrene Kranich, Lydia Shelford, Beatrice Watson, Mabel Svedlund, Mrs. Faulk, Bonnie Bowers, Bidig Waddell, Gladys Watson, Ann Sholin, and Laura Frazier plus one unknown.

Helen and Dick Edens Mothers Day 1940.

Thelma and Harris Gordon sitting on the steps to their log cabin.

Esther Anderson (two unidentified) Jane Harrington Lillian Walli and Alfred Anderson.

Mae Harrington's daughter, Jane.

Pa Crittendon in door way. Jane and Mr. Schaffer. (Pa Crittendon was MaeHarrington's Father)

Mae Harrington's son Jack.

To the left Marion Anderson with daughter Elizabeth; both drowned in a boating accident as did baby Alieen.

Above Helen and Dick Edens at the Homestead, 1939.

Harris and Thelma Gordon on board the ship for Alaska with young Garen and the twins Joyce and Joan. 1936.

Roland Lee above the mouth of Fritz Creek. Photo by Bill Waleland.

Bob and Arleen Kranich with sons Bill and Ray.

George Kirkpatrick.

Joyce Christensen, now, Kirkpatrick with baby geese. Walt's mail truck behind.

Nils Svedlund, commonly know as "Pa" and Mable Schotter Svedlund, know as "Ma".

Charley Miller & Pa Svedlund.

Oscar, Mamie, Stanley, and Alice Woodman.

Came to Alaska in 1937. Stanley Woodman at the time, 16, skiing at the homestead.

Stanley and George Dahlgren bear Hunting.

Grandmother Mamie Woodman with Alice (now Bellamy) with children going to church.

Sam Pratt posing with a painting he painted and presented to the new school. Left is Vega, behind Howard Mayhill and on the right is Arlene Kranich and Mrs. Chapman.

Bob Kranich and Arlene with boys Bill & Ray for a Christmas Party.

Sam Vega Pratt at the same Party.

1936 Steve Zowistowski
building the boat
"Normandy"
Now part of the Pratt
Collection.

Carl and Ann
Sholin's son Bob.

Lillian Walli
with new
husband
Pat Miller,
Manager of
the Control
Tower of
the first
Homer
Airport.

Wilma Cowgill, Helen
Alm, and Natalie Hewlett.

These nurses provided
medical care to the resi-
dents of Homer for years.
Their skill and caring, during the period before the
care that we all have
today surely makes them
Homer Pioneers.

THE MINUTES OF
THE HOMER CIVIC LEAGUE

The Minutes of the Homer Civic League most clearly demonstrated the plans and concerns of these Pioneer Spirits.

The Pratt Museum has the Mae Harrington cabin on it's Grounds to honor her outstanding contribution of time and effort.

Walt Christensen, the man on the cover, showing us where Homer is, came to the country in 1932; at eleven years old he and his sister Pearl started right out being the janitor and general helper at the only tiny one room school and Walt would spend the rest of his life helping others while also working for his living. Always modest—always cheerful. Sam Pratt was the idea man and Walt the man who was always there to lend a helping hand. There were many others in Major projects like Bob Kanich, Carl Sholin, Charley Miller, to name a few more specifically involved where Walt stepped in to any and all projects.

He died in 1999, two months after I had interviewed him. At 88 he was supplying the Ninilchik Senior Center with meals and other needs. Always helpful and if prased would just laugh.

HOMER CIVIC LEAGUE MINUTES

March, 27, 1937	January 9, 1939	January 6, 1940
November 13, 1937	February 6 1939	February 5, 1940
	March 6, 1939	April 1, 1940
	April 1, 1939	April 7, 1940
April 22, 1938	April 3, 1939	April 15, 1940
April 23, 1938	April 4, 1939	May 18, 1940
April 24, 1938	May 1, 1939	September 4, 1940
November 7, 1938	June 27, 1939	November 11, 1940
November 11, 1938	September 11, 1939	December 1, 1940
November 16, 1938	October 4, 1939	December 5, 1940
December 5, 1938	November 6, 1939	December 12, 1940
		December 15, 1940
		February 10, 1941
		March 10, 1941
		April 7, 1941
		May 5, 1941
		October 4, 1941
		October 14, 1941
		November 3, 1941

Transferred from note book received by Mae Harrington,

Secretary, Homer Civic League, original book on file.

March 7th, 1937.

****

       Community Meeting Aug. 27

Motion made and seconded to elect chairman and secretary in
open meeting.

          Mr. Berry for Secretary
          Tom Shelford   Chairman
          Guy Waddell

     (Mr. Berry elected Secretary
     (Tom Shelford elected Chairman
     (Kronich
     (Waddell   <u>three chairman</u>
     (Miller

          Chas Miller 34 Guy Waddell 23
          Mr. Kronich   45
Nominations   Jack Deitz   21
          Forslund   12

       ****

Mar 29 – Standing vote for community to build dock –
       Unanimous.

       Motion made to have Civic League have charge of
       building dock – carried.

       ****

Directors Meeting called Sept. 18, 37 and decided that each
       phone owners repair an allotted amount of line &
       posts.

Also decided to build the line on the hill, the people on the
       hill to do all the work & to be allowed to join the
       line on the same conditions as other phone owners
       $10.oo initial payment and 5.oo each <u>succeding</u> year
       until $25.oo has been paid in, the phone company to
       furnish the wire and insulators.

       Prince William Sound Power & Light Co., Valdez.
             12 or 12 battery type phone

       Sent loo.oo for wire insulators
       brackets & 2 post hole diggers.

       ****

Nov. 13, 1937.

Meeting of Homer Civic League called & attended by the community
        Election of new radio phone operator taken by ballot.
        Dale Peugh elected.

****

(STRUCK OUT Feb. 24 - 1938)

Meeting held Feb 17, '38. Meeting of Homer Dock Association called.

Motion made & carried that Dock Association pay one half of the
        grub bill while CCC cutting the piling.

Motion made and carried that ballot vote be taken to decide whether
        a limit on dock payment or shall be unlimited. Unlimited
        won by majority. Unlimited 27.   Limited 4.

Motion made & carried that solitors be appointed to collect money
        for dock. H.K.Allen appointed hill solicitor, Dale Peugh
        appointed for Valley and Jim Waddell for the east side.

Motion made and carried that residence in the community be estab-
        lished for thirty days or become a property owner before he
        has a vote.

Motioned made & carried that we adjourn at 9:33 p.m.

****

SPECIAL MEETING HELD APRIL 22, 1938.

A Special meeting of The Homer Civic League was held at the Walli Hall, Thursday April 22, 1938 with Thomas Shelford in the chair with fifty seven members present.

The secretary A.W.Berry resigned and M.A.Berry was appointed secretary protem.

The minutes of the last meeting were read and it was moved and seconded that "Motion made by George Kirkpatrick last meeting be stricken from the records. Motion carried.

The proposed by laws for The Homer Civic League were read by Arleen Kranich. It was moved and seconded for Article 1 Sect. 11 to read "in any public meeting place" voted upon by raising of hand and accepted as the "Ayes have it".

Article II Sect. 1 - II - III. Article accepted as read.

Article IV Sec. 1. 1-2-3-4 accepted as read. Motion made and carried to add Report of Treasurer as Sec. 5, Sec. 6 motion made & carried to include a reading of Roberts Rule of Parlimentary Drill at Regular and Special Meetings. Sect. 7 - 8 - 9 - lo - 11 - 12 approved as read.

Article V Sec 1. Motion made to strike out "citizen" from Sec. 1 It was moved & seconded that we accept as read and carried.

Article VI Sec. 1 - 2 - 3 - 4 - 5- 6 - 7 . It was moved and amended to read "Official Bill Boards" moved, seconded and carried that we accept Article as read.

Article VII Sec. 1 - 2 - 3 - 4 - 5 - 6 - 7 - 8. It was moved that we accept Article as read and carried.

Article VIII. It was moved & seconded & carried that we accept Article 8 as read.

Article IX. It was moved, seconded & carried that we accept Article as read.

Article X. Moved, seconded and carried that we accept article as read.

Article XI. Moved, seconded and carried that we accept Article as read.

Article XII. Dissolution of League. Motion made & seconded that Art. 12 be made to read "that any funds left be used as remaining members decide thereon. Motion carried.
It was moved and seconded that Constitution be accepted as corrected and Amended as a whole. Carried

It was moved that we elect three new officers to hold office until next Regular Meeting.

54 votes were cast: Berry 32   Harrington 32   Forslund 42

Motion was made & seconded that the Civic League pay Mr. Murphy for the use of the tractor to come out of the dock fund. 35 yes   7 no.

It was moved and seconded that bill of groceries used by volunteers aiding in piling and moving lumber be paid by Civic League. Yes 41 No 1.   Kranich Volunteers 34.56 other grocery bills 38. 04.

Motion made and seconded that we adjourn at 1:15 a.m. Apr. 23.

Thomas Shelford resigned from t.e Chair.

****

Civic League Meeting.

The regular meeting of the Homer Civic League was held
at Wallis Hall Monday, November 7, 1938, with the President in the
chair and Haleen Ingalls acting as Secretary. There were 38
members present.

The minutes of the previous meeting were read and approved.

The Treasurer's report showed a balance of $43.12 in the
dock fund, $21.o2 in the telephone account and a balance of $lo.45
derived from miscellaneous sources. The report was accepted.

A telegram from Delegate Dimond pertaining to the WPA work
was read by the Secretary.

The years report of the Board of Directors wasread and also
a list of the projects suggested for WPA work.

Mr. Ingalls and Mr. Monroe were appointed tellars.

A motion was made seconded and voted that the Board of
Directors be offered a vote of thanks for their services for the
past year.

The nominations to elect three members of the Board for a term
of one year were in order. There were 37 votes cast and the
following five were nominated: Mr. Miller, Mr. Race, Mrs. Harrington,
Mr. Forslund and Mr. Kronich.

The following 3 were elected for a term of 1 year, Mrs.
Harrington 29, Mr. Forslund 23, Mr. Kronich 27.

During the nominations to elect 4 members for a term of 2
years the following 5 were nominated, Mr. Miller, Mr. Race, Mr.
G.Waddell, Mr. Sholin and Mr. Brandvold. The following 4 were elected
for terms of 2 years, Mr. Sholin 24, Mr. G. Waddell 31, Mr. Race
28, Mr. Miller 29.

There were 26 votes cast during the nominations for 3 alternate
those nominated were Mr. Monroe, Mr. Ingalls, Mr. Allen, Mr. Brandvold, Mr. Matheson and Mrs. Hansen. The following 3 were elected,
Mrs. Hansen 21, Mr. Monroe 19 and Mr. Allen 11.

There were 28 votes cast during the nominations for 2
Auditors the following 5 were nominated. Mrs. Fraxier, Mr. Ingalls,
Mrs. Kranich, Mrs. Forslund, Mrs. Berry. The 2 elected were Mrs.
Kranich 22 and Mr. Ingalls 17.

A motion was made, seconded and voted for adjournment.

Haleen Ingalls
Sec. ptotem
11/8/38.

BOARD OF DIRECTORS MEETING.

The Regular monthly meeting of the Board of Directors was
called to order by the President at 8-30 p.pm Oct. 7, 1938.

The following members were present: Mae Harrington, Robert
Branich, Lloyd Forslund, Chas. Miller, M.A.Berry.

The minutes of the last meeting were read & approved.

The motion was made & carried that we order five telephones
instead of six also one hundred brackets & insulators.

It was moved and seconded that we pay small bills to the
extent of $83.85.

It was moved and seconded that we write letter to the
Alaska Steamship Co. regarding the boat docking at Homer Dock.

The motion was made & carried that posters be made asking
for applicants for watchman, stating price and qualifications also
to ask people who are interested in a cooperative doctor fund.

The motion was also made that we write for information
towards getting WPA work & funds.

It was moved & carried that we write Mrs. Mildred Hermann
& Dimond about getting a hospital here.

It was moved that we adjourn at 11-15 p.m.

Inga Hansen

Alternate acting Secretary.

REPORT of PRESENT BOARD OF DIRECTORS
OF
HOMER CIVIC LEAGUE
****

November 7th, 1938.

We, the Board of Directors of the Homer Civic League present our report of business done by us since our first meeting held April 24th, 1938.

According to the by-laws we held an election among ourselves and the following officers were elected:
President, Mae Harrington
Vice President, Charles Miller
Secretary, Maybelle Berry
Treasurer, Robert Kranich
Lloyd Forslund
Guy Waddell, consiting of six members.
We posted notices for a public meeting for the election of a seventh member to replace Thomas Shelford, resigned, but for lack of aquorum this meeting could not be held, we have, therefore, been conducting the affairs of the League with a membership of six, with the required quorum of five.

The following committees were appointed:
Dock Committee: Guy Waddell, Chairman
N.O.Svedlund
A.W.Berry
Don Ingalls
H.K.Allen

Telephone Committee: Charles Miller, Chairman
Jim Waddell

Cemetery Committee: Mae Harrington, Chairman
Glen Bowers
Charles Erickson

We have ordered and received two telephones, one for the Spit and one for Miller's landing. The CCC have built the line from the end of the Spit to the main line and a phone will be installed at the end of the Spit in a few days. Through courtesy of one of these phones have been laoned to Mr. McCroskey for the summer. We have also ordered five more phones for those who have requested them.

According to the Treasurer's report we have paid to Mr. Murphy of Seldovia for the tractor the sum of $181.00.

Correspondence was carried on the Alaska Road Commission and as a consequence and as a result the road to the Spit has been made so that trucks may now go to the dock for freight.

A request has been made to the Commissioner of the General Land Office for the $N\frac{1}{2}NW\frac{1}{4}$, $SW\frac{1}{4}NW\frac{1}{4}$, $NW\frac{1}{4}SW\frac{1}{4}$ Section 22 to be set aside for an air plane landing, as yet we have received no reply.

Letters of thanks and appreciation have been written to Mr. Carl Johnson and Mr. Jack Anderson for thei help and assistance in constructing the dock.

Application of 71 residents of Homer have been forwarded
to Governor John W. Troy for WPA work to be done here. Several
projects were recommended. We are in receipt of the following
telegram from Anthony J.Dimond, our delegate, in answer to our
letter for assistance in this matter. Read telegram.

A telegram and a letter have been sent to L.W. Baker,
Traffic Nanager of the Alaska Steamship Company asking that all
Home freight be rebilled to Homer directly instead of to Seldovia
as has been previously. The S.S?dordova arriving about November 18th is
expected to discharge freight at Homer.

A letter has been written to Anthony J.Dimond asking his
assistance in getting a government doctor placed here or for assistance he may be able to give us.

In reply to a letter of October 7th from H.J.M.Baker,
Senior Rngineer of the War Department we have protested the extension of the Anderson Dock at Homer Spit for three years, for the
reason that our dock is finished and it is necessary for another
one on Homer Spit. At the same time we asked for a permit for 200
feet to extend our dock and to build an ice shear. We sent a wire
as well as a letter to support this project.

A Trade and Manufacturing Site has been applied for containing about 3 acres adjacent to and west of the dock to build
warehouses, offices etc. that will be necessary to carry on the
business connected with the dock.

We thank you and appreciate the confidence you have
placed in us, and hope that in some small way we have shown that
your confidence has not been misplaced, our one project of which
we may all be doubly proud is the completion of our dock and
we take great pleasure in turning ir over to the League.

> Mae Harrington
>
> Charles Miller
>
> Lloyd Forslund
>
> Robert Kranich

BOARD OF DIRECTORS.

A meeting of the Board of Directors was held at Mrs. Harrington's house, Nov. 11, at 6 p.m. with the President in the chair. Six members were present also Mrs. Hansen, an alternate for G.Waddell. The minutes of the last meeting were read and approved as corrected.

Mr. Kronich read the treasurers report w ich was accepted as read.

It was moved, seconded and voted to take the telephone from school house and install at Homer Dock.

Moved, seconded and voted that the telephone ring for the Dock be 2 longs, Mrs. Kholer to continue using her ring.

An election forofficers of the Board of Directors was held with the following results:

Mr. Forslund elected President, receiving four votes.

Mr. Miller elected Vice-President, four votes.

Moved, seconded and voted that the vote be cast unaniamously for Mrs. Harrington for Secretary. Mrs. Harrington accepted.

Moved, seconded and voted that the vote be csst unan iously for Mr. Kranich for Treasurer. Mr. Kranich accepted.

Moved, seconded and voted that the present chairman continue with the meeting. Mr. Forslund to take the chair at the next meeting.

Moved, seconded and boted that all vacant land from "Slough" to beach available for aviation field, comprising 479.41 acres be leased, the fee of $1o. to be sent to land office.

Moved, seconded and voted that the Secretary write to Dept. of Commerce for specifications of emergency field and regular aviatic field.

Moved, seconded and voted that the Secretary write to Mrs. Hermann of Juneau to secure information about Liabilities and Incorporating the Homer Dock.

Moved, seconded and voted that for the time being the Secretary check the freight at her responsibility at the Dock payment ior such services to be considered at a later date.

Moved, seconded and unanimously voted that the temporary dockage rates be one dollar more than Seldovia rates, on general merchandise per ton and other freight raised accordingly in the same ratio. For districts outside ofnHomer, the Seldovia rates to prevail.

Moved, seconded and voted that the Secretary notify outside communities on the dockage rates at Homer.

RESULTS

OF THE

ELECTION OF THE

BOARD OF DIRECTORS OF

THE

HOMER CIVIC LEAGUE,

HELD

NOVEMBER 7, 1938.

****

Waddell, Guy (31)	Miller, Charles (29)
Harrington, Mae (29)	Race, Lloyd (28)
Kranich,Robert (27)	Sholin, Carl (24)

Forslund, Lloyd (23)

****

ALTERNATES

Hansen Inga (21)	Monroe R.L. (19)

Allen, H.L. (11)

****

AUDITORS

Ingalls Don (17)	Kranich Arleen (22)

****

BOARD OF DIRECTORS MEETING.

****

The meeting of the Board of Directors was called to order by the President at 3-20 p.m. Sept. with the following members present, Mae Harrington,Robt Kranich, Lloyd Forslund, Chas. Miller and M.A.Berry.

The minutes of the last meeting were read and approved.

The motion was made & carried that Forslund be allowed to take telephone to his place & try it out until needed for the Dock. It was moved and seconded that we order six telephones for the community.

The motion was made and carried that we sell about two hundred feet scrap telephone wire to Gilbert Sanford which is now on slough road for the sum of one dollar.

It was moved that telegrams paid for by Shelford & Berry totaling six dollars twenty five cents be reimbursed by treasury funds.

The motion was made by Sidney V.Dennison & carried that we write letters of thanks to Jack Anderson and Carl Johnson, for their aid towards the Homer Dock.

The motion was made by Robert Kranich 7 seconded that we adjourn at 4-20 p.m.

> Maybelle Berry
> Secretary.

Five telephones were ordered instead of six as was mentioned.

> Inga Hansen
> Read and approved
> Nov. 11, 193

BOARD OF DIRECTORS MEETING.

****

Meeting of Board of Directors held on April 24, 1938, 2 p.m.

Moved and seconded that vote of Forslund (1) Mae Harrington (5) be accepted and was unanamously elected President.

Moved & seconded that we accept Chas. Miller as Vice President (3) carried.

Vote taken for Secretary Mrs. Berry (4) Kronich (1) moved that we accept Mrs. Berry unanamously accepted.

For Treasurer Kranich (3) Forslund (2). Moved that we accept Kranich as Treasurer. Accepted as Treasyurer.

Motion made by Robt Kranich that we hold a meeting (public) on First Monday in May 2. moved and seconded. carried unanamously to elect seventh officer on board and make a treasurers report and a report on Projects.

Motion made by L.Forslund, moved and seconded that the Board of Directors have thepower to borrow money at a legal rate of interest to meet bills which may come in and ca ried unanamously.

Moved & seconded that the secretary write a letter asking for a road to the Spit to connect with the dock.

Moved and carried that we appoint a committee to handle the management of building the dock with Guy Waddell as Chairman, N.O.Svedlund, A.W.Berry, Don Ingalls & H.K.Allen.

Moved and seconded that we appoint a Cemetary Committee with Mrs Harrington as Chairman and Glen Bowers & Chas. Erickson on comm.

Moved & seconded that we appoint a telephone committee of two Charles Miller for east side Jim Waddell west side to see that line kept in order. Carried.

Moved & seconded that we write for prices on printing loo phamphlets on By Laws of Homer Civic League. Carried.

Moved, seconded & carried that we order two telephones and write for prices on steel outdoor phones for use, one at Miller's Landing, one at Spit and one ay Beach.

Motion made by Forslund & carried that we rite Alex Matheson giving size & printing of Homer Civic League Seal triangular in shape with emblem in center pertaining to Homer about 1½" diameter.

Motion made by Forslund & carried that we notify Mr. Lipke th any telegrams from the Civic League will be signed by M.A.Berry Secretary and countersigned by the President and any messages for the Civic League may be sent as regular radiophone message, also notify postmaster at Homer to deliver all mail pertaining to Homer Civic League to M.A.Berry.

Motion made & seconded that we adjourn at 5.15 p.m. Carried.

Maybelle Berry, Secretary.

Moved, seconded and voted that the Secretary have notices posted on the official billboards for applications for watchman on dock, such bids to be returned by midnite of Nov. 15.

Moved, seconded and voted that the meeting be adjourned. Adjourned at lo-lo p.m.

Inga Hansen
Secretary Protem.

****

BOARD OF DI.ECTORS.

Meeting called to order by President, Lloyd Forslund, at the home of Carl Sholin at 2 p.pm. Members present Lloyd Forslund, Mae Harrington, Robert Kranich, Charles Miller, Lloyd Race, Carl Sholin and Alternate R.L.Monroe, November 16th, 1938.

Minutes of the previous meeting read and approved as read.

Report of telephone committee accepted.

Secretary reported on correspondence received in re WPA Motion, made, seconded and accepted that we wait for an answer to our last letter before any further action being taken.

Motion made, seconded and accepted that the letter in re to printing of b laws be takbled, and that Secretary typewrite a few copies for the time being.

Motion made, seconded and accepted that the application as made b Secretary for lease of certain sections for an airport be mailed. Ten dollars and a quarter were authorized paid by the Treasurer to cover the fees requested by Land Office.

R.M.Campbell and Frank Wolfe, president and treasurer of the telephone committee on the hill made proposition to buy 8 rolls of telephone wire on hand, payments made by Kranich and Haarsted $lo. each to apply on bill.   Balance to be paid at a furure date. Insulators and brackets to,be lent until others ordered are received to replace borrowed ones.   Proposition voted upon and accepted.

Motion made, seconded and carried that Secretary send a wire to Anthony J.Dimond, Del. from Alaska, Wash. D.C. in re to mail boats discharging mail at the dock. Also information about plane carrying mail.   The following telegram was dispatched on board S.S. Cordova cost $3.15.

"Night Letter.

Homer, Alaska, Nov. 23, '38.

Anthony J.Dimond
Delegate from Alaska,
Washington, D.C.

Please confer Farley regarding delivery of all Homer mail at dock by Fern or any other mail carrying vessel. Homer freight billed in Seattl direct no necessity extra mail service between Seldovia and Homer. Als during winter months airplane service is offered Ninilchik, Kasiloff and Kenai wny not include Homer.

Homer Civic League
by M.Harrington, Sec.

Sealed bids on the Watchmans job at the end of the Spit read and discussed.

Ole Haarstad reC8d	12-30 p,pm.	11/15/38.		$60.00
Lee Wisdom "	11-55 am	"		$150.00
Alberson J.A. "	11-1o "			$59.85
Erickson Chas. "	13pm/	11/13/38		$50.00

An ananimous vote was cast for Charles Erickson.

Dory for use at end of Spit was offered by Lloyd Race.

Time of watchman to begin from day he takes over the job. Lloyd Forslund donated paint for trucks.

Chas. Miller appointed as a committee of one to get dory from Don Ingalls.

Motion made and accepted that letters be written to collect outstanding telephone bills.

Mrs. Matheson paid initial payment for telephone right. L.Forslund paid $7.50 for his telephone.

Meeting adjourned.

Mae Harrington
Sec'y.

Approved as read.

* ****************

BOARD OF DIRECTORS.

Meeting of the board of Directors of the Homer Civic League called to order by the Presidnet Lloyd Forslund at 7-30 pm December 5, 1938, those present were Charles Miller, Lloyd Race, Guy Waddell, Carl Sholin and Mae Harrington, December 5th, 1938.

Minutes of the previus meeting read and approved as read.

The following bills were presented and approved, payment voted.

N.O.Svedlund	board bill on piling project 3/23/38		9.20
" "	" with CCC		31.00
W.Murphy on tractor			35.00
Freight bill for tim from Sears Roebuch & Co.			16.88

made by motion, seconded and carried.

Mr. Miller report that the dory could be used, but ithas been claimed by Mr. Sarakovakoff in Seldovia.

The chair appointed the following committees:

Motion to adjourn made, seconded and carried at 1 p.m.

Mae Harrington
Secretary.

Correction: Order eight phones instead of three.

****

BOARD OF DIRECTORS.

Meeting called to order at 7 p.m. January 9th, 1939, at the home of Mae Harrington, by the President Lloyd Forslund. Charles Miller, Guy Waddell, Lloyd Race other members answered roll call, there being a quorum of 5 members.

Minutes of the previous meeting read and approved as read.

Lloyd Forslund reported that he had paid Carl Anderson and Dick Sheard $2. each for longshoring on Cordova November 24th, 1938. He also reported that he had interviewed Mrs. Berry in regard to wharfage rates and it was satisfactory with her.

Secretary reported the payment of $5o. to watchman Charles Erickson December 18th, 1938. Also $2. for wire sent to War Department December 20th. Wharfage collections were $63.0a for December trip of Cordova. Secretary reported receipt of $25. from Pete Nielsen in payment of note for dock fund. Motion made, seconded and carried that bill for Homer Cash Store for $9.3o foroil used while cutting lumber and that $25. be sent to W.J.Murphy on tractor.

Motion made, seconded and carried that a letter of thanks be sent to the Homer Woman's Club for the donation of $70.00 which they tendered toward the dock indebtedness.

Motion made, seconded and carried thata letter of thanks be sent to N.O.Svedlund for gavel presented by him to the Legue as a Christmas present. Secretary was instructed to write to General Electric Co. and Delco Co. in regard to electric apparatus for heating and lighting dock.

A letter from Ninilchik Welfare Committee was read in regard to blazing trail from Homer to Ninilchik. Motion made, seconded and carried that a wire be sent to the Committee as follows:
"We approve trail blazing project and have requested Dennison's help"

and that a letter be written to Sidney V.Dennison for help by CCC boys.

Secretary instructed to write about liabilities to insurance company and that letter from Mrs. Hermann be laid on the table until answer be received from the insurance company.

Motion made, seconded and carried that Mr. Svedlund be asked to make desk for dock office.

Motion made, seconded and carried that we buy a fire extingusher for the dock and two fillers.

Motion made, seconded and carried that the League give a card party January 14th, 1939, the proceeds to be used for dock fund.

Motion to adjourn at 1o pm.

Approved as read.   Mae Harrington, sec.

Dock: Guy Waddell and N.O.Svedlund
Cemetery: Lloyd Race, Alfred Anderson and Glen Bowers
Telephone: Charles Miller, Jim Waddell.

Report on the wharfage for the freight from S.S.Cordova Nov.
24th, 1938, showed $79.76 amount collected.

Motion was made, seconded and carried that the following
rates be made for livestock:

Horses $5.   and colts under 1 year $2.50
Cattle $4.   " calves   " " "   2.00
Sheep $1. each regardless of age, except a small number
           oflambs that might be born on shipboard.

Motion made, seconded and carried that the consignee must
pay all expenses for stock after discharged from boat, until delivery.

Motion made, seconded and carried that Mr. Forslund, make
a settlement with Bobb Walli, Carl Anderson, Don Sheard, Leonard
Jackson and Dick Sheard for longshoring, but not to pay more then
$2. each.

Motion made, seconded and carried that the longshoring be
done by volunteers until a further date. Guy Waddell, Carl Sholin
& L.Forslund volunteered and L.Race and Mr. Miller if they could.

Motion made, seconded and carried that the Secretary write
and ascertain the fee for insuring the dock for $3500.00.

Motion made, seconded and carried that we wait for reply
from insurance company before funds are set aside for insurance and
reserve.

Motion made that the Treasurer pay the watchman on the 18th
of each month. No second and after discussion was withdrawn.

Motion made, seconded and carried that the Secretary have
a fund on hand of $75., $50. to be paid to the watchman and $25.
for petty cash to be used as change and pay any freight collect, the
balance over and above $75. to be turned over the Treasurer.

Secretary port receipt of $lo. initial payment on telephone
right from Grover Price.

Motion made, seconded and carried that we send for 3
telephones and to get information about number that can be on line
in order to have good service.

Motion made, seconded and carried that the C C C 's be
asked to put a railing on dock when they build the warehouse.

Motion made, seconded and carried that a sign be printed and
placed in a glass frame stating that we do not assume any responsibility for damages or accidents to any person on dock.

The Chair suggested that Alex Matheson be asked to make the
frame.

L.Forslund was delegated to interview Mrs. Berry and Carl
Sholin the Homer Cash Store in regard to two different wharfage prices,
before patrons were solicitated.

BOARD OF DIRECTORS.

Meeting called to order at 7;20, February 6th, 1939, at the residence of Charles Miller, othersmembers present Lloyd Forslund, Guy Waddell, Carl Sholin, Lloyd Race, and Mae Harrington, making a quorum of six members, president presiding.
Minutes of the previous meeting read and approved.

We had as quests M.C.Edmonds, Supt. of the Alaska Road Commission, Thomas L.Shelford, Foreman WPA project and Don Ingalls.

Secretary reported that the receipts of the wharfage for the S S Cordova on January 26th, 1939, was $1o7.01, less $1o. paid to Charles Lange through Berry Store and $11.65 paid to Homer Cash Store for damaged mayonnaise, leaving a balance of $85.36. Also reported the receipt of $31.05 proceeds from Card Party after the expenses of $1o.65 had been deducted. An accumulation of $23.30 from the dance receipts was turned over to the Dock Fund by the Community. It was decided that this be kept in a separate account for telegrams etc. that may come up for the community.

A C.O.D. parcel at the post office was ordered withdrawn and paid amounting to $11.86, these supplies being for the office consisting of books, etc.

Letters were read from the following by the Secretary:
Land Office in re T. & Manu. Site, order for survey
War Department in re to Dock Extension and Ice Shea
Land Office   "   " application for Airport Lease.
Sears Roebuck   "   "   seal for Civic League.
M.C.Edmonds, A.R.C. in re. to road work at Homer.
Motion was made, seconded and carried that these letters be answered as necessary.

Motion was made, seconded and carried that the Phamphlet as written by John M.McAnerhey, Instructor in Geology, be copied and posted in both stores, to ascertain the numbers of residents who would be interested in taking the course.

Motion was made, seconded and carried that the Sevretary send a telegram to the American Automatic Electric Sales Co., Seattle, Washington, in regard to the delay in receiving the two shipments of telephones ordered from them.

Motion was made, seconded and carried that we write to Sidney V.Dennison, Head Ranger C C C , Seward, Alaska, asking him to build a ramp at the beach end of the dock, we to furnish the materials, said ramp to be 12 x 50 feet.

Motion made, seconded and carried that we buy two riding lights for the dock.

Motion made, seconded and carried that $15. due Thomas L. Shelford for hauling dock timbers and tow, be paid.

After listening to a snort talk by Mr. Edmonds, it was decided that we write to the Road Commission requesting a survey for the road on the hill for a distance of about tan miles. Meeting was adjourned at 1o-1o p.m.

Mae Harrington
Secretary.

BOARD OF DIRECTORS.

Meeting of the Board of Directors was held at Carl
Sholin's residence on March 6th, 1939, at 8:30 p.m. with the
President inthe Chair. Lloyd Forslund, Charles Miller, R.L.
Kranich, Carl Sholin and Mae Harrington answered roll call,
making a quorum of five members present.

Minutes of the previous meeting read and approved.

Secretary reported the receipt of $70. 00 from the
Homer Woman's Club and the payment of $50. 00 to the watchman
at the dock.   She also reported that the lines had been run for
the ice shear and the Trade and Manufacturing Site on the Spit.

Motion made, seconded and carried thatthe balance due
W.J.Murphy on the tractor and for timbers used in the dock be
paid, said amount being $40.70; $168.50 to be paid said W.J.
Murphy by the Territory of Alaska, upon the recommendation of
Sidney V.Dennison.

Motion was made, seconded and carried that the cable
borrowed by us from Tore Lund to make the temporary ice shear
last month and which was carried away by the ice,be replaced,
being 300 feet of ½ inch cable.

Meeting was adjourned at 1o-40 p.m.

M. Harrington
Secretary.

****

FINANCIAL REPORT OF THE HOMER CIVIC LEAGUE
FROM November 6th, 1937 to April 1, 1939.
****

CASH RECEIPTS.

```
Cash receipts 43 individuals @ $25. ------ $1075.
  "      "    3     "    part pay. ----     29.
             Total amount received               $1558.88
```

EXPENDITURES.

```
Nov. 6,'37 to Aug.10,'38, initial cost lumber $618.60
Aug. 10,38 " Apr. 1,'39  general payments      881.54
             Total cash paid out                      $1500.14
             Cash on hand                                 58.74
                                        $1558.88  $1558.88
```

From the total amount of expenditures the sum of $66.70
was spent on incidentals leaving a total of $1433.44
paid out on account of the dock.

WHARFAGE ACCOUNT.

```
Wharfage collected during November    $79.76
   "      "        "     December      63.01
   "      "        "     February     107.01
                        March          52.42   $302.20

         Paid for longshoring           4.
         Morgan freight collect        17.21
         Damaged mayonaise             11.65
         A.R.C. freight collect        12.04
         Watchman's salary            200.00           244.90
              Bal. to dock fund                         57.30
                                       $302.20  $302.20
```

Amount paid from general fund for telegrams $30.26

ACCOUNTS RECEIVABLE.

```
Morgan freight charges collect  $17.21
A.R.C.    "      "       "        12.04
Individual notes                 196.      $225.25
```

ACCOUNTS PAYABLE

```
N.O.Svedlund          $179.70
R.B.Malone              11.
H.S.Young                3.50
Charles Lange           10.
M.A.Berry (plus sheet iron)  7.
Homer Cash Store        47.45      $258.65
```

TELEPHONE ACCOUNT.

Balance received from Maybelle Berry	$43.37	
Cash received payments on tele.rights	35.	
" " for telephones	60.	
L.M.Moore 252 ft wire	.75	
6½ rolls wire @ $6. to hill telephone	39.	$178.12

Sears Roebuck & Co.	12.		
Ame.Auto E. Sales	91.		
Wharfage, stamps, M.O.Fees	1.21		
Telegram to A.A. E. Sales	2.65		
Refund Kronich & Haarstad	20.	$126.96	
Balance cash on hand		51.16	
	$178.12	$178.12	

Respectfully submitted

Mae Harrington
Secretary.

--HOMER CIVIC LEAGUE MEETING.--

The regular semi-annual meeting of the Homer Civic League was held in Walli's Hall on the first Monday in April, the third, 1939, at 9;20 p.m.

The meeting was called to order by the President, Lloyd Forslund, 28 members being present.

The minutes of the previous meeting were read and approved as read.

The report of the Board of Directors for the past five months were read. Motion was made and seconded that report be accepted as read. Carried.

The report of the telephone committee by Mr. Miller was accepted.

The dock committee reported that the warehouse on the dock was completed and that the CCC boys were now getting piling for an ice shear and extension tothe dock.

The cemetery committee had nothing to report on account of the weather hindering them from doing anything.

The treasurer's report was read by the Secretary in place of the Treasurer who was absent.

The auditor's reported that they had examined the books and found them in good shape.

Motion made and seconded that the Secretary write for the League to the Alaska Aeronautics Comunication's Commissi n at Juneau, Alaska, asking that techinian be sent to overhaul the radio phone, motion carried.

Motion made and seconded that the Board of Directors circulate a list for donations to be presented to Frank Beers, radio phone operator for his services, for which he received no compensation. Motion carried.

Motion made and seconded that Sevretary get all information about cost of privately owned radio set, operating regulations and licenses.   Motion carried.

Letter from Virginia Mason Hospital in regard to doctor read. Motion made and seconded that we write directly to the interne recommended asking upon what conditions he would come up here, explanning the situation thoroughly and getting his viewpoint. Carried.

Motion made and seconded that the Board of Directors attend to the matter of getting the piling up into Mud Bay and getting chains for securing them. Carried.

The matter of a cold storage as suggested was laid on the table, upon a motion being made, seconded and carried.

Moved and seconded that we adjourn at lo-55 p.m.

Mae Farrington.
Secretary.

BOARD OF DIRECTORS MEETING.

A meeting of the Board of Directors of the Homer Civic
League was held at Charles Miller's residence April 4th, 1939,

Meeting was called to order by President Llyod Forslund
at 7-30 p.m. Roll call showed five present, Forslund, Miller,
Waddell, Sholin and Harrington.
Minutes of the previous meeting read and accepted as read.

Letter from the surveyor read and Secretary was instructed
to get more information on the subject.

Motion made and carried that we buy warehouse on Spit from
Raby, Guy Waddell to pay what ever was asked up to $40. and to
make arrangements. Carried.

Motion made and seconded that the bill to Charles Lange for
clearing the airport for the plane to land with Edmonds carried.

Motion made and seconded that the collection for the radio
operator be made in the fall when the amounts received would be
larger as there would be more money. Carried.

Motion that bill be sent to Dick Scott for collection of
freight bill for Lew Morgan. Carried.

Motion made and seconded that the watchman and bookkeeper
as they are, the watchman receiving $50. per month and the book-
keeper $25. from the month of November until the first of September.
Carried.

Motion that the Secretary see Mrs. Schultz and also write
to the Red Cross about getting an emergency kit. Carried.

Motion made, seconded and carried that we adjourn at 12-15.

Mac Harrington
Secretary.

approved.

REPORT OF BOARD OF DIRECTORS
OF THE
HOMER CIVIC LEAGUE.

April 3rd, 1939.

We, the Board of Directors of the Homer Civic League present
our report upon the business transacted by us since the meeting held
November 7th, 1938.

WE elected Lloyd Forslund, president,
Charles Miller, vice president,
R.W.Kranich, Treasurer,
Mae Harrington, secretary.

The president, Lloyd Forslund appointed the following standing
committees:
Dock; Guy Waddell and N.O.Svedlund
Cemetery: Lloyd Rage, Alfred Anderson and Glen Bowers
Telephone: Charles Miller and Jim Waddell

Letters of thanks have been written to N.O.Svedlund for the
gavel presented to the League as a Christmas gift, and to the Homer
Womand's Club for the donation of $70.oo made by them to the dock fund.

We have paid to the account of W.J.Murphy for tractor and lumber
the sum of $281.70. which balances our account with him to date, the
remainder to be py by the Territory of Alaska through Sidney V.Dennison,
superintendent of the CCC.

We advertised for and selected as a watchman Charles Erickson
at the salary of $50.oo per month, who has been filling that position
since November 18th, 1938.

On account of our application for lands to be leased as an
airport conflicting with the Homestead Entry of John Kohler, we have
made an amended application, and as yet have received no reply to the
application.

In reply to our request for information about getting a doctor
here we have received one reply.

We received no favorable results to our application to the
Legislature for a hospital which was probably due to the fact that one
was appropriated for Seldovia.

We have written for information and are negcitating for insurance
to be placed on the dock, in case of fire and also damages and liabilities

We have bought one large fire extinguisher for the dock.

A petition has been circulated by us for signers who wish to
take the mining course given by the University of Alaska through John
M.MCAnerney,instructor, and have received 29 applications, the month
of December being selected as the most convenient for all concerned.

A request has been sent to the Alaska Road Commission to make
a survey of the road on the hill for a distance of lo miles for the
convenience of new comers so the, can build their trails accordingly.

The lines have been run and marked for the ice shear and the
Trade and Manufacturing Siteon the spit and posts put in where necessary.

Our petiti n to the Post Office Inspector asking that the mail be delivered to the dock instead of seldovia was rejected. We are taking the matter up with Anthony J.Dimond, our delegate and as yet have received no reply.

The books of the league have been audited and certified to by the Auditors, Don Ingalls and Inga Hansen substituting for Arlene Kranich.

Respectfully submitted,

Lloyd Fortune

Guy Waddell
Chas. Miller
Mae Harrington

BOARD OF DIRECTORS MEETING.

A meeting of the Board of Directors of the Homer Civic League was held May 1st, 1939, at the home of the Secretary, Mae Herrington. Those present were Lloyd Forslund, Charles Miller, R.W.Kranich, Carl Sholin, Mae Harrington, with Frank Wolfe as guest, and Guy Waddell coming late. Quorum of five.

The minutes of the previous meeting were read and approved as read.

Carl Sholin reported that the ramp at the dock had been completed. Report accepted.

Bob Kranich reported that the piling was in Mud Bay, also that Brososky had been hired to secure logs for safe keeping and that Charles Lange was to snipe the piling for $10.oo. Accepted.

Secretary reported the receipts for wharfage as $86.04 and $95.29, making a total of $181.33 for month of April. Accepted.

Guy Waddell came late so minutes were read over for his benefit.

Secretary also reported that the wharfage of Lew Morgan and the Alaska Road Commisson had been paid.

Motion made that Charles Miller hire someone to repair Spit telephone line. Seconded and Carried.

Carl Sholin made the proposition that he would repair the line and receive as compensation his last payment on telephone right, accepted.

Motion that we write the Better Business Bureau and the American Automatic Electric Sales Co. about the telephones. Carried.

Secretary reported that cable for Tore Lund had arrived.

Motion that the sum of $25. for warehouse be sent to Frank Raby. Carried.

Guy Waddell reported that Murphy would haul the piling for 50 cents each .

Motion that we pay mr. Svedlund $12. for desk. Carried.

Motion that we adjourn at 11-30 p.m.

Mae Harrington
Secretary.

approved

BOARD OF DIRECTORS MEETING.

June 27 39

A meeting of the Board of Directors of the Homer Divic League was held at the home of the Secretary Mae Harrington on June 27th, 1939. Charles Miller, Vice President presided, and others present were, Robert Kranich, Carl Sholin, Guy Waddell, Inga Hansen, Harry Allen, Lloyd Race making a quorum of 8 members.

Minutes of the precious meeting read and approved as read.

Report of Carl Sholin that Charles Lange could not snipe the piling and that someone else would have to be hired. Motion made to that effect, seconded and carried.

Letter was read by the Secretary from the American Automatic Electric Telephone Co. whereby they returned $91.oo we had sent them for old telephones.

Motion made that money orders be cashed and money refunded to those who had made a deposit for phones, so that they could buy their own phones. Seconded and carried.

Motion that the bill to Sears Roebuch & Co. for $2.93 and to Mrs. Young for $3.50 be paid. Seconded and carried.

Letter from Dr. Stagg from Ketchikan was read

and motion made that details be written to him about the situation
here.   Seconded and carried.
Motion that we write to the Governor and Medical Board
asking for an appropriation or some help for a hospital, and that
Secretary write a personal letter to Anthony J.Dimond about the
matter. Seconded and carried.
Motion that a bill be sent to the Alaska Road
Commission for wharfage charges. Seconded and carried.
Motion that we adjourn.

Mae Harrington
Secretary.

BOARD OF DIRECTORS.

Regular meeting of the Board of Directors held September
11th 1939 at the home of the secretary and was opened at 5-30 by President
Lloyd Forslund. Other officers present R.W.Kranich, Lloyd Race, R.L.
Monroe, Carl Sholin and Mae Harrington, quorum of 6.
Motion made that we pay for longshoring at the rate of $1. per
hour preference being given to those who have volunteered in the past
or dock members. Seconded and carried.
Motion made that the following bills be paid:

Ray Malone	$11.00	
N.O.Svedlund	24.00	Graham piledriver men.
Wm. Murphy	55.70	
N.O.Svedlund on acct.	79.70	

Seconded and carried.
Motion made that we accept and pay for the stove ordered by
N.O.Svedlund when it arrives. Seconded and carried.
Motion made that we buy enough galvanized iron to cover the
old warehouse after it ismoved, for an eight foot entension to the
present one, plasterboard liningfor office on the installment plan from
SearsRoebuck & Co., Seconded and carried.
Motion that we adjourn at lo-lo p.m.

Mae Harrington
Secretary,

Correction: Motion made that Mae Harrington draw the balance due her for
services as harfinger from November 24th until September 24th1939
said amount being $175. Seconded and carried.

BOARD OF DIRECTORS.

Meeting of the Board of Directors held at the home of
Mae Harrington, Secre ary, and called to order at 7.30 October
4th, 1939, by the President Lloyd Forslund, others present Charles
Miller, Carl Sholin, Inga Hansen, a quorum of 5 members.
Minutes of the previous meeting read and approved as
corrected.
Motion made that the following bills be paid:

Jack Deitz	$50.
Dave Murphy	loo.
S. Jones	50.
Vincent	20.
Miller	11.81 Total $231.81

seconded and canried.
Motion that Carl Sholin see Gus Naslund about buying skiff
for $20.oo, Seconded and carried.
Motion that Carl Sholin get piling in slough. Seconded and
carried.
Motion that vote of thanks be given to Frank Beers for
stool donated to the Dock office. Seconded and carried.
Motion that we write a letter of thanks to Carl Johnson
for his help with the pile driver. Seconded and carried.
Secretary reported the sums of $5. each from Lloyd Forslund
and Alex Matheson, also $4.30 for J.R.Crittenden as payments on
telephone rights.
Motion that Bert Hansen be allowed to work for payment of
telephone right in lieu of receipt lost. Seconded and carried.
Motion that Messrs Forslund and Frazier be allowed $3.
each for work on the Spit telephone line, same to apply on their
telephone right. Seconded and carried.
Motion that another petition be circulated for hospital
building and equipment to the amount of $20,000. Seconded and carried
Motion made that we write to the Post Office Department
about be included on the route of the new boat running to the
westward. Seconded and carried.
Motion that the question of livestock received on small
boats paying wharfage the same as large boats be laid on the table.
seconded and carried.
Motion that we adjourn at 12.15 October 5th, 1939.

Mae Harrington
Secretary.

Meeting of Board of Directors.

Meeting called to order at 7;45 at the residence of the
secretary by the President Lloyd Forslund, other members being present,
Mae Harrington, Charles Miller, Guy Waddell, Carl Sholin and Inga
Hansen, alternate for Lloyd Race, making a quorum of six.
Minutes of previous meeint read and approved as read.
Treasurers report as given by the secretary accepted.
Secretary report the price of treated piling.
Motion made that we write about WPA work for the coming winter
or spring. Seconded and carried.
Motion that we replace the cable of Mr. Miller's used on the
dock, same being 130 feet, 3/8 in. Seconded and carried.
Motion that the reduction in wharfage charges be laid on the
table. Seconded and carried.
Motion made that that the rules be suspended and that the officers
now serving, namely, Lloyd Forslund, President, Charles miller, Vice
President, Mae Harrington, Secretary, R.W.Kronich, Treasurer, xxdx
be anaminously elected for the same offices for the following year.
Seconded and carried.
Motion that the two barrels of oil bought from the Standard
Oil Co. in Seldovia, 2 barrels be paid. Seconded and carried.
Motion that N.O.Svedlund be paid $50., Murphy $35. Jones 20.
Seconded and carried.
Motion athat Carl Sholin see Garen Svedlund about cutting timber
for warehouse. Seconded and carried.
Motion that we adjourn at 12;30.

____
Secretary.

****
M EETINg of board of directors.

Meeting called to order on January 6th, 1940, at 7:30
p.m. at the home of the Secretary, by President Lloyd Forslund.
Other members present Charles Miller, Guy Waddell, Carl Sholin, Inga
Hansen, quorum of six.
Minutes of the previous meeting read and approved.
Report of funds on hand accepted.
Lloyd Forslund reportedthat pile driver was finished and
on the dock.
Motion that a record be made of the working time on dock
with the untilmate outcome of payment at some time in future, at CCC
wages or better, when money is available. Seconded and carried.
President appointed Guy Waddell and Mae Harrington to
interview Mr. Putnam about engine and belt from Glen Bowers.
Motion that Carl Sholin interview both stores about bill of
grub for workers. Seconded and carried.
Secretary instructed to write Farms Rehabitatinn Board about
loans to foarmers.
Motion thatwe adjourn.

____
Secretary.

REPORT OF BOARD OF DIRECTORS
OF THE
HOMER CIVIC LEAGUE.

November 6th, 1939.

We, the Board of Directors of the Homer Civic League present our report upon the business transacted by us since the meeting held April 3rd, 1939.

We have paid to William J. Murphy the sum of $55.70 which was overlooked by Sidney V. Dennison, Chief Ranger, Forest Service, and therefore our duty to pay.

No definite report has been made by the Land Office in regard to the Airport except that they requested our Constitution and By-Laws, which was duly forwarded.

We have been unable to come to any final arrangements in regard to a Doctor being located here. At this time we have in circulation a petition which are asking the residents to sign and which will be sent to our Representative Ed. Coffey to be presented to the coming Session of Alaska Legislature in January for the appropriation of a hospital and equipment. Many Doctors are willing to come but they all want a hospital ready for their convenience.

A permit has been granted us for the erection of an extension to our dock of 64 feet, putting in a dolphin and ice shear. This permit expires December 31st, 1942.

As the M S Fern is to be taken off the westward run we have asked the post office department to include Homer in the route of the boat which will be substituted for the Fern.

We have purchased the old warehouse at the end of the dock from Frank Raby for $25. the same to be moved and placed alongside the dock and refloored and covered.

The money received from the American Automatic Electric Telephone Co. has been given to those making a deposit for their phones.

It was decided by the Board that from the first of September that the longshoring be paid for at the rate of $1. per hour preference being given to those who had donated longshoring or were dock members.

Letters of thanks have been sent to Frank Beers for the donation of an office stool, and to Carl Johnson for the use of the pile driver.

On August 25th, 1939, we sent a telegram to W.A.Hesse Highway Engineer as follows: Funds depleted before school road finished stop will you appropriate fifteen hundred dollars answer respectfully Homer Civic League, and received the following reply August 26th: Additional fifteen hundred dollars authorized for Homer school road today. Hessee.

It was decided that the wharfinger was to receive $25. per month from the twenty-fourth of November until the 24th of October the sum of $275.00.

The books of the league and dock have been audited and certified to by the Auditos, Don Ingalls and Arlene Kronich.

Respectfully submitted,

____
President

____
Vice President

____
Treasurer

____
Secretary

____

____

Minuted of the Regular Meeting of the
Homer Civic League, Held November 6th, 1939.

Meeting called to order at the Homer Territorial School
building at 8 p.m. November 6th, 1939, by President Lloyd Forslund,
Other members present, Mae Harrington, Secretary, Robert Kranich
Treasurer, Charles Miller Vice President, Guy Waddell, Carl Sholin,
Minuted of the previous meeting read and approved as read.
Treasurer's report read and it was moved and seconded and
approved that report be accepted as read.
Report of Charles Miller on telephone line received and
approved.
Motion that the cold storage question be tabled until
more money was on hand. Carried.
Report on the dock was given by the wharfinger and motion
that same be accepted, seconded and carried.
Report of Board of Directors, and approved by motion duly
seconded and carried.
Motion that the report of Thomas Shelford on the dock
be accepted, seconded and carried.
Discussion of radio phone donations. After motion that
committee be appointed to make collections, upon learning that
Womans Club had already appointed a committee, motion was withdrawn.
Motion that Womans Club be responsible for collections for
radio phone operator, seconded and carried.

Election of officers by ballot.

Nominations for three:

		Elected:	
Forslund	31	Forslund	37
Kranich	23	Kranich	32
Harrington	27	Harrington	24
Jim Frazier	6		
Don Ingalls	5		

Nominations for alternated:

		Elected:	
Inga Hansen	20	Inga Hansen	32
R L Monroe	15	R L Monroe	27
Don Ingalls	12	Don Ingalls	32
Frazier	9		
Bunnell	6		

Nominations for Auditors:

		Elected:	
Arlene Kranich	24	Arlene Kranich	33
Laura Frazier	9	Laura Frazier	22
M Berry	6		

Motion that chair appoint a committee to met and discuss
and present at the meeting in April amendments for membership.
Committee: Sam Pratt
Jay Tolbert
Laura Frazier
Mae Harrington
Lloyd Forslund

Motion that committee consider the 1st monday in November
and April at 1 o'clock. Seconded and carried.
Motion that Mr. Putnam go with some of the members of the
Board to the dock and if they find any piling that are marked with
Putnams initials the League to replace them. Seconded and carried.
Letter read by Mr. Kronich from Mr. Dennision.
Motion that Mr. Putnams letter be held until he and the

members of the board have made their examination. Seconded and
carried.

Motion that we amend the by-laws so that residence
be changed from six months to ninety days. Seconded and carried.

Motion that we adjourn.

Mrs Harrington
Secretary.

Meeting of Board of Directors.
————————————————

Meeting called to order on April 15, 1940, at 7:30p.m. at the home of Chas. Miller, by Pres. L. Forslund. Other members present Guy Waddell, Carl Sholin, Don Ingalls, Robert Kranich, Inga Hansen, a quorum of seven.

Minutes of the previous meeting read and approved.

Carl Sholin reported that Chas. Chestnut wuold act as wharf- inger, and Chas. Erickson would continue as watchman, with a reduc- tion in pay.

Moved, seconded, and carried that Garen Svedlund be paid twenty-five dollars on account due him.

Moved, seconded, and carried that a meeting for Dock Members be held at the Cook Inlet School, on Aprll 28, at 2:00 p.m. Secretary to mail cards to those persons who might not see notices. Discuss results of petitions and what steps should be taken as to maintain Dock.

Meeting adjourned at II:30 P.M.

Inga Hansen
Secretary.

****

Meeting of Board of Directors, held May 18 th. 1940.
————————————————

Meeting held at the home of Mrs. Berry. Called to order at 8p. m. by Chas. Miller, acting chairman. Other members present R. Kranich, Guy Waddell, Carl Sholin, Don Ingalls, Inga Hansen, a quorum of six.

Minutes of the previous meeting read and approved.

Moved, seconded, and voted that the secretary write a letter of thanks to Mr. Hesse, in reply to his, advising us that they would fur- nish creosote piling for the Dock.

Moved, seconded, and voted to accept contract leasing a cannery site to Mr. Barnhill, the Homer Civic League acting on behalf of the Dock Association. The secretary has filed a copy of the Lease.

~~Meeting adjourned at II:00 p.m.~~ *minutes continued*

Meeting of Board of Directors.

Meeting called to order at 8 p.m. on February 5th,1940,
t the home of the Secretary, Lloyd Forslund, Carl Shloin, xxxxxRobert
zasenh Guy Waddell, Charles Miller and Mae harrington being present,
aking a quorum of 6.
Minutes of the previ s meeting read and approved as read.
Report of Lloyd Forslund on his trip Seldovia, Alaska,
or engine for pile driver received and accepted, and the following
ills approved:

Expense of Lloyd Forslund	$20.oo
Hauling Lars Sagen	40.oo
Garner & Williams, mechanics	17.oo
Messages, Seldovia Radio	4.oo
Seldovia Cash Store, rope	4.75

Joe Hill for magneto $45.oo or $45. for useof
engine to M$_1$lo Hurlburt.
Motion that report be accepted and bill be paid when
ossible, seconded and carried.
Motion that $4.75 be paid to Wm. Putnam for battery
nd wire. Seconded and carried.
Motion that we adjourn at 11/15 p.m.

Mae Harrington.
Secretary.

rrected: Robert Kra ich present
in place of Inga Hansen.

Me eting of Board of Directors.

Meeting called to order by the President at 8 p.m.
arch 18th, at home of Secretary Mae Harrington.
Roll Call, Lloyd Forlsund, Charles Miller, Inga Hansen,
on Ingalls, Carl Sholin, Robert Kranich and Mae harrington, quorum
f seven.
Minutes of previous meeting read and corrected,
obert Kranich being present instead of Inga Hansen.
Report of Lloyd Forslund on trip for piling. Pete Nielsen
o receive $5. ior the trip. Upon motion seconded and carried $5.
as appropriated for Pete Nielsen for the trip.
Motion that a flat rate of $.75 be paid by consignees
n oil or gasoline for wharfage, per drum, empties free of charge.
econded and carried. No change made on wharfage for dynamite or
xplosives.
Motion that the Captain be asked to save the freight
nd make one trip a monthly unless the freight warrants more trips,
ut to be assured of one trip per month, instead of landing the
reight in Seldovia,. Seconded and carried.
Mae Harrington requested an alternate during her absence.
Motion that I$_n$ga Hansen be appointed as Secretary.
econded and ca ried.
President appointed Carl Sholin to see Charles Erickson
nd Charles Chesnutt in regard to watchman and wharfinger jobs on dock.

Motion that we adjourn.

MM Waddell
Secretary.

PIONEERS OF HOMER

Report of Board of Directors
of the
Homer Civic League.

April 1st, 1940.

We, the Board of Directors of the Homer Civic League present our report upon the business transacted bu us since the regular meeting held November 6th, 1939.

An estimation of the piling need for repairing the dock wase sent to the West Coast Wood Preserving Co., and they gave us aprice of 49¢ net per linear foot f.a.c. Seattle, wharfage for buyer's account, payment within 30 days.

On response to our telegram to Anthony J. Dimond in regard to borrowing money from the R.F. C. we received a rather lengthy letter, which will e read upon the request of the meeting.

We have written a letter to M.C.Edmunds, Supt. Alaska Road Commission, recommending roads etc. for the coming year, and have been assured thatwe would receive our quota of the appropriation and were very glad to learn that Peter Bagoy would be returned as road foreman.

A letter addressed to Governor Gruening in regard to securing reduction of rates on shipments on stock, machinery, farm implements etc. on freight charges, was answered by E.L.Bartlett Acting Governor who advised us that the matter had been referred to the Alaska Steamship Company.

We have been advised by A.C.Kinsley, field man for the Land Office that our Trade and Manufacturing Site on the Spit is in good order and that it will not be necessary to have it surveyed, until we are financiallly able and desire to prove up on the Site.

In response to our inquirey as to whether the Farms Rehabilitation Board had extended the Farm Security Administration to Alaska, the answer was in the negitative, it has not been extended to Alaska as advised by H.E.Drew Director.

We wish to thank the CCC boys for tearing down thd rebuilding the warehouse on the dock, it is now ready for the iron as soon as it arrives.

We also wish to thank all those who have helped in reppiring the dock, with the piledriver or any other work connected with the work; as the result of their labors the dock is int condition for docking the steamers. We have requested the Captain to save the freight and assure us of one boat a month, or if the freight warrants more then one trip; but if the freight is saved for one trip per month we avoid having to pay the extra freight charges from Seldovia to Homer.

A petition for a hospital was sent to Governor Gruening but as yet we have received no answer.

The books of the wharfinger and treasurer have been audited and found in good order.

_______________________________   _______________________________

_______________________________   _______________________________

_______________________________   Mae Harrington _______________________________

Minutes of the Regular Meeting of the
Homer Civic League, Held April Ist. I940.

Meeting called to order at the Cook Inlet School at
p.m. April Ist; I940, by Pres.L. Forslund. Other board members
resent,R. Kranich, Osholin, C. Miller, L. Race, D. Ingalls, and
nga Hansen acting as Secretary.

Roll Read, one member ~~shot~~ lacking for regular quorum.
Motion that we continue with meeting, seconded and carried.
Treasurer'sreport read and it was moved seconded and
pproved that report be accepted as read.

Minutes of the previous meeting readdand approved as read.
Report of Board of Directors read,and approved by motion

conded and carried.

Report on proposed ammendments read.

Moved,seconded,carried that a committee be named to
ork on any new ammendments and to accept and offer any suggested
mmendments made to them singly by persons to this committee
henever they meet and to prsent proposed ammendments at next
egular meeting. Committee named:

Geo. Earle   Maybelle Berry   L. Forslund
Don INgalls   Robert Kranich

Mr. Swanson,representing the Kenai Dev. League spoke
n ways and means of obtaining a Doctor for Homer.

Moved, secondedand carried thatt acommittee be named
to work in conjunction with the Kenai Dev. League to canvass
for funds to help support a Doctor. Committee:

Vilma Matheson   Walter Christensen   L.Forslund.

Motion that we adjourn at Io:30 p.m.

Inga Hansen
Secretary.

MEETING OF DOCK MEMBERS ----APRIL 7, 1940.

A meeting for Dock Members was called at the
Kachemak Bay School on April7, at 2P.M. Mr. Forslund
called the meeting to order. Discussion was held as to
ways and means of obtaining money to repair Dock.

It was agreed to offer to the Public the following
propositions to be voted upon:

Proposition number One: All in favor and willing to
buy $25.00 or more stock in incorporated dock or sign Notes
promissory notes payable on or before September Ist.
Vote yes by signing name below.

Proposition number Two: All in favor and willing
to pay $Io.oo per ton wharfage for the next eight months
so that dock pay for it's own piling.

Proposition number Three: All in favor and de-
siring to have their freight discharged at Seldovia beginning next fall when Dock goes out and regular boat service
is discontinued.

Copies of the above propositions were to be distributed as
follows; One copy at the Homer Cash Store; one copy at the
Berry Store: Mr. Kranick to take one copy on the Hill; Mr.
Bunnell one copy on the Hill; Mr. Ingalls one copy for the
East Side: Mr. Hansen one copy for the West Side.(Same
copy in postoffice for week.
Meeting adjourned at 4P.M.

Meeting of Board of Directors on May I8, continued:

Moved, seconded, and voted that the wharfage rates on out-going freight be reduced and the following rates prevail:

One dollar and fifty cents$(I.50) per Ton.

Fifty cents ($.50) minimum.

Moved, seconded, and voted that we adjourn at II.00 p.m.

Inga Hansen
Secretary.

****

Meeting of Board of Directors on Sept.4, I940.

— Sept.4ʰ

Meeting called to order at 8p.m. by Mr. Forslund at the home of Mrs. Hansen, acting secretary. Other members present were C. Sholin, D. Ingalls, C. Miller, R. Kranick, quorum of 6.

Minutes of previous meeting read and approved as read.

Moved, seconded, and voted to pay Mr. Hulbert one hundred and seventy-five dollars for engine on driver.

Moved, seconded, and voted that we apply to C.C.C. for repair work on Dock and warehouse.

Moved, seconded, andvoted to send order to Sears and Wards for material to complete warehouse and repair Dock.

Meeting adjourned at II:I5 p.m.

Inga Hansen
Secretary.

****

Meeting of Board of Directors held Sept. I8th, I940.

Meeting called to order at 8p.m. at the home of the secretary,with Mr. Miller as acting chairman. Other members present, D. Ingalls, C. Sholin, R. Kranick, quorum of five.

Minutes of previous meeting read and approved as read.

The secretary reported sending $I75.00 to Mr. Hulbert, $I35.00 to Sears, and $I6.00 to Wards.

Moved, seconded, and voted to get rope from Monroe, and replace in near future.

Mr. Cambell was invited to attend this meeting and for him to proceed with work as outlined.

Semi-annual meeting of the Homer Civic League.

The regular meeting of the Homer Civic League was called to order at 8 p.m. in the Woman's Club Hall on Nov. II,1940, by Mr. C. Miller, acting chairman.Other directors present were Don Ingalls, Guy Waddell, Carl Sholin, R. Kranick, Inga Hansen, acting secretary.

At the opening of the meeting, fifteen persons paid their annual membership fee of twenty-five cents.

The treasurer's report was read, and moved, seconded, and voted to accept as read.

The secretary read the report of the Board of Directors, which was accepted as read.

The auditors, Mrs. Frazier and Mrs. Kranick, reported that they had audited the books, and found them in good order.

Mrs. Matheson reported that the majority of the people were in favor of contributing towards a fund to help obtain a Doctor here.

It was moved, seconded, and voted that the minimum rate on small packages, carried by the local boats, should be twenty- five cents.

It was moved, seconded, and voted to raise the pay of the watchman ten dollars a month, making it a total of thirty- five dollars at the present time.

The two amendments that had been advertised were vated and accepted as amended. Since the amendments are in the prvious meeting minutes, they are not being re-read as they are quite lengthy, but any one may read them upon request. They have also been to the constitution.

It was moved, seconded, and voted to post-pone the election of officers until Dec. Ist; at that time Dcck Members and League members would be asked to be present. The present Board of Directors would take care of any business until that date.

Motion for adjournment was made at IO:60 p.m.

Inga Hansen, Sec.

Minutes of special Dock and Civic League Meeting held Dec. Ist.

Meeting called to order in the Club Hall, at 2p.m. by **Mr. Miller,** he then asked to have someone else in the Chair.

Motion made, seconded, and voted that Mr. Ingalls be chairman.

Minutes of the previous meeting read and approved as read.

Moved, seconded, and voted to elect a Dock committee of three, with one alternate, to take care of Dock business.

Nominations for Dock committee:

Dale Peugh	Frank Beers
R. Kranick	C. Erickson
R. Campbell	Guy Waddell

Elected:

D. Peugh I2; G. Waddell I2; R. Kranick 8; C. Erickson 8;

Moved, seconded, and voted that Mr. Kranick be the regular member, and Mr. Erickson the alternate.

The wharfinger's report read, and accepted as read.

Moved, seconded, and carried that we nominate Civic League officers from the floor.

Nominations for Directors:

Walter Christeson	G. Waddell	Jim Frazier
Sam Pratt	**Mrs. Berry**	Jim Waddell

Elected for a term of two years:

J. Frazier I2; W. Christeson II; G. Waddell II; J. Waddell II

Elected for one year: Sam Pratt IO.

Moved, seconded, and voted that the present auditors, Mrs. Frazier and Mrs. Kranick be re-elected. Vote was unanimous.

Nominations for alternates:

Mrs. Pratt; Mrs. Matheson; Mr. Miller; Frieda Berry.

Alternates elected for one year:

Mr. Miller I2; Mrs. Pratt II; Mrs. Matheson IO.

Motion for adjournment at 3:30 P.M.

Secretary.

Meeting of the Board of Directors Dec. 5, 1940. 8:30 P.M.

The meeting was called to order at the home of Guy Waddell, by acting Chairman Robert Kranich. The minutes were read and approved.

Officers were elected by a unanimous vote as follows:

    Jim Frazier,   President
    Robert Kranich   Vice-President
    Walter Christensen Secretary-Treasure

Motion made and carried that a letter of appreciation be sent to Mr. Edmunds containing a request for enough maintainance funds to widen and put guard rails at all dangerous dips and curves in the road allready completed.

Motion made and carried that 50 insulators and 50 brackets be returned to the Hill telephone Co. in return for supplies borrowed from them by the C.C.C's for use on the telephone line.

Motion made and carried to order 100 lbs. wire, 50 brackets, and 100 insulators from Telephone Co. funds.

Motion made and carried to order telephone for dock warehouse from Telephone Co. funds.

Motion made and carried that board meet with Dale Peugh Dec 15 at the home of Jim Waddell to discuss ways and means for building a community hall and clubhouse.

Meeting adjourned at 10:05 P.M.

Walter Christensen Sec

approved as read

Meeting of The Board of Directors Dec.12, 1940 7:30 P M.

The meeting was called to order by President Jim
Frazier, at the home of Jim Waddell. The minutes were read and
approved.
Ways and means were discussed for the building of
a community hall
Motion made and carried that Ole Peugh draw up a
modefied version of the small building displayedand present it
to a community meeting Dec. 1 called for that purpose.
Meeting adjourned at 10:15 P M.

Walter Christensen Sec.

Community Meeting   December 15 1940   4:15 P.M.

The meeting was called to order by President Jim Frazier at theWomens Club Hall, to discuss the building of a community hall. There were 21 persons present.

There was lengthy discussion on the matter but no motion was made.

Motion made and carried that the Civic league write the Board of Education of the need of a new and larger school house equipped with a gymnasium and other necessary conveniances

Motion made and carried that the Civic League circulate a petition to raise money to pay for medicine and supplies used by the district nurse while in Homer

President Frazier asked Vice-president Kranich to take the chair, at 5:00 P.M.

Motion made and carried that the Civic League make a subscription list for the compensation of the radio-telephonn opperator. It was suggested this list be left in a prominent place for 30 days and then circulated from house to house.

Motion made and carried that the Commissioner be wired about the plight of Frank Nemic, and advise that the case be taken care of immediately as his condition is serious.

The meeting was adjourned at 5:30 P.M.

Walter Christensen Sec.

Meeting of Board of Directors, Feb.10,1941. 9:45 P.M.
The meeting was called to order at the home of W.J.Frazier.
The minutes were read and aproved.

Motion made and carried to buy enough plywood to make two buletin boards to be placed one at each store.

Motion made and carried to write Mr.Malcolm for information conserning their plans for keeping a nurse in Seldovia; also their arrangements for paying their doctor.

Received notice from Land Office to withdraw application for our trade and manufacturing site or pay $400 for survey. Motion carried to notify land office of inability to pay for survey, but of wish to retain trade and manufacturing site.

Meeting adjourned at 11:45

Walter Christensen Secretary

MEETING OF THE BOARD OF DIRECTORS. MARCH 10,1941. HOME OF SAM PRATT

The meeting was called to order at 8:30 P.M. by Vice-president Kraniah. The minutes were read and approved.

The motion was made and carried to write D.L.Reynolds, supervisor of the Alaska Aironautic and Communications Commission requesting repairs for the Radio telephone.

Motion made and carried to write Almer J. Peterson in regards to getting funds for building a recreational hall in Homer.

Meeting was adjourned at 10 P.M.

Walter Christensen, Sec.

April 7-4,

Semi Annul Meeting of the Civic League, April 7, 1941, Womens Clubhal

The Meeting was called to order by Pres. Frazier, at 7:40 P.M. There were 15 members present.

The Motion was made and carried that we transact such business as we had on hand without the necessary quorum.

The Minutes were read and approved.

Received notice from public health service that Homer would be included in the nursing scedule providing we raised $300 to secure the Federal Grants-in -aid before May 1.

Motion made and carried to circulate a list to raise the necessary funds.

Motion made and carried to write Mr. Parks, head of the G. L. O. Survey, for information as to wheather E. D. Calvin surveyed the Civic League's trade and Mfg. site.

Motion made and carried that a committy be named to draw up an amendment to Article VI. Sec.1, of the Civic League Constitution and by laws, concerning the percent of membership necessary for a quorum.   *Mrs Kranich and Mrs Hansen were named*

Meeting was adjourned at 9:30 P. M.

Report of the Board of Directors April 7, 1941

We the Board of Directors of the Homer Civic League
Present our report of the business transacted by us since
the regular meeting of Dec. 1st, 1941.

A letter of appreciation was sent to Mr. R.C. Edmonds,
containing a request for the improvement of the bad spots
in our present road.

Additional supplies were ordered for the Telephone Co.
part of which were returned to the Hill Telephone Co. for
equipment used on our line by the C.C.C. gang. A telephone
was ordered to be put in the dock warehouse.

A letter was sent to the Commissioner of Education,
stressing the need of a larger school building equipped with
a gymnasium, at the Cook Inlet School.

A Radio telephone Subscription list was made for the
compensation of the radio telephone opperator. The returns
amounted to $75.50.

Two new buletin boards were put up for Civic League
notices.

Mr. Malcolm in Seldovia, was writen for information
regarding the financing of their government nurse, and their
prospective doctor.

Received notice from Land office to withdraw application
for our trade and mfg. site or pay $450 for survey. A letter
was writen informing them that we were unable to raise the
nacessary funds, and if said funds were absolutely necessary,
to consider the application withdrawn.

A letter was written to D.L.Reynolds A.A.& C.C. requesting repairs for the radio telephone.

Almer J Peterson, Alaska Legislature, was written with
regards to getting funds for building a recreational hell in
Homer.

MEETING OF THE BOARD OF DIRECTORS, MAY 5 1941, Home of JoyceChristensen

The meeting was called to order by President Frazier at 8:15 P.M. The Minutes were read and approved.

The motion was made and carried that we write the general passenger agent of the Alaska Steamship lines, in Seward, requesting that they make Homer a by-monthly port of call.

The motion was made and carried to write James C. Ryan, Commissioner of Education as to the possibility of consolidation of the Homer Schools.

Motion made and carried to write Mr. Coffee a similar letter thanking him for his help in securing our new school building.

the meeting was adjourned at 10:40 P.M.

Secretary.

Oct. 4 –

Meeting of Board of Directors Oct 4, 1941. Home of Jan Prat[h]

The meeting was called to order by President Frazier at 8.15 P. M.

The minutes were read and approved.

Motion made and carried to make a list to be left at the stores, to collect the ballance of the pledged contribut[e] for the Public Health Nurse.

Motion made and carried to write Mr Edmunds concernin[g] his plans for winter road maintainance.

Motion made and carried that material used in installing the School telephone be replaced by the telephone Co.

Motion made and carried that a workman be hired to repair the Homer telephone line. Cost not to exceed $40.

Meeting adjourned at 9:55 P. M.

Walter Christensen, Secretary.

Special meeting Board of Directors oct 14, 1941.

Meeting was called to order by President Frazier at 7:10 P. M.

It Had been brought to the attention of the board that a piece of land leased by the Homer Civic League some time previously, was embraced in the plot selected by the government for a government airport.

The board was given notice that if this was not relinquished it would hold up the construction as much as ninety days.

Acting in behalf of the Civic League, President N. J. Frazier, Secretary Walter Christensen, and board members Guy Waddell and Sam Pratt, Constituting a quorum of the board, signed a relinquishment of said lease.

Motion made and carried that a hundred insulators be purchased for the Homer telephone Co.

Meeting adjourned 8:20 P. M.

Walter Christensen Secretary

Minutes of Civic League Meeting Nov 3, 1947.

The meeting was called to order by President W. J. Frazier. The minutes of the previous meeting was read and approved. The treasure's report was given and found satisfactory.

The motion was made and approved that W. G. Putnam be allowed $10 on his telephone account for work done on the telephone line.

Motion made and carried that a dock meeting be called for Nov 17.

The annual Election was held. Directors elected to replace outgoing members Lloyd Farslund, W. J. Frazier, R. W. Kranich, and Jim Pratt, are as follows:

Norman Ellis, 14 Votes, Jim Pratt, 13, Pete Nielsen 13, and Frank Beers 10.

Alternates elected were: Vega Pratt 11votes, Inga Hansen 9, and Rhina Bowers 8.

Auditors elected were Laura Frazier 13, and Inga Hansen

Meeting adjourned at 11:00 P. M.

Walter Christensen, Secretary.

Nov 3-41

Report of Board of Directors Nov 3 1941

We the Board of Directors present our report of all business transacted since the regular meeting of April 7. 1941

A letter was sent to Mr Parks. G. L. O. Survey for information concerning the survey of the ~~survey of~~ Civic League Trade and Mfg. Site. No Answer has been received.

A letter was written the Gen Pass. agent Alaska SS Co requesting more regular ~~service~~.

A letter was written commissioner Ryan of the possibilities of a consolidated school in Homer.

Twelve dollars worth of telephone supplies have been ordered for the telephone Co.

~~Hired~~ G Workman ~~Geo Bowers~~ to repair telephone line. Received & paid bill for five days ~~spent~~ work of man and his car, at $8.00 Per Day.

N Christensen Secretary.

Honorable Discharge
from the
Civilian Conservation Corps

TO ALL WHOM IT MAY CONCERN:

This is to Certify That * ROBERT W. KRANICH

a member of the CIVILIAN CONSERVATION CORPS, who was enrolled

NOVEMBER 29, 1937 at HOMER, ALASKA , is hereby
(Date)

HONORABLY DISCHARGED therefrom, by reason of **

CAMP TEMPORARILY CLOSED IN ANTICIPATION OF OPENING OF FISHING SEASON

Said ROBERT W. KRANICH was born in GREAT FALLS

in the State of MONTANA When enrolled he was THIRTY-THREE years

of age and by occupation a FARMER He had --- eyes,

--- hair, --- complexion, and was --- feet

--- inches in height. His color was WHITE

Given under my hand at JUNEAU, ALASKA , this FOURTH day

of MAY , one thousand nine hundred and THIRTY-NINE

____
(Name)   (Title)
Acting Regional Forester

* Insert name, as "John J. Doe."
** Give reason for discharge.

C. C. C. Form No. 2
April 5, 1937

RECORD OF SERVICE IN CIVILIAN CONSERVATION CORPS

**Served:

a. From ___9/18/39___ to ___1/31/40___, under ___F.S. AGRI.___ Dept. at ___HOMER, ALASKA___

Type of work ___LEADER___ *Manner of performance ___GOOD___

b. From _______ to _______, under _______ Dept. at _______

Type of work _______ *Manner of performance _______

c. From _______ to _______, under _______ Dept. at _______

Type of work _______ *Manner of performance _______

d. From _______ to _______, under _______ Dept. at _______

Type of work _______ *Manner of performance _______

e. From _______ to _______, under _______ Dept. at _______

Type of work _______ *Manner of performance _______

Remarks: _______

PAID IN FULL BY CHECK NO. 43539 $76.00

M. J. LYNCH
CCC SPECIAL
DISBURSING AGENT

FEB 24 1940

JUNEAU, ALASKA
STA. NO. 4__

FINAL STATEMENT NO. 5219

Discharged: ___JANUARY 31, 1940___ at ___HOMER, ALASKA___

Transportation furnished from _______ to _______

Ray Ward
(Name)   (Title)

Acting Regional Forester

*Use words "Excellent", "Satisfactory", or "Unsatisfactory".
**To be taken from C. C. C. Form No. 1.

U S GOVERNMENT PRINTING OFFICE   3—10171

NAME INDEX PIONEERS OF HOMER, ALASKA

Allen Lyman
Alien, Pop 70-71
Aim, Helen 94-95
Anderson, "Missy"
Anderson, "Papa" Jack Sr. 16-17
Anderson, Aileen
Anderson, Alfred 28, 29,
. 45
Anderson, Ed 29
Anderson, Fred 29,66
Anderson, Gus 12,27
. 45,66
Anderson, Jack Jr. 17
Anderson, Juanita
Anderson, Margaret 16
Anderson, Squeaky 26,90
Anderson, Thelma
Anderson, Vega . . . . .prefix v
Anderson, Virgo
Amess, Jim 17
Bagoy, Pete 58
Banks, Delia Murray 4, 85
Becker, David & Eileen . .61
Bellamy, Ben 66
    Don 66
    Raymond 66
    Marvin 66
    Benny 66
    Linda 66
    Kenny 66
    Judy 66
Bennett, Mr. 70
Berger, Heinie 16
Bernard, Bud 55
Berry, Arthur & Maybelle .16, 57
Bretts, The
Bird, Ernest 30
Boltoa, Electa 4
Bowers, Bennie 12, 13,
. 29
Bowers, Glen 12, 13,
. 29

Bowers, Phina 12, 13,
. 29
Bradley, J. A. 4
Branch, Eva
Broderson, Erling 65
Bunneff, Mr.
Burger, Heinie
Burroughs, Jon 8
Byers, Lee 88
Christensen Family
Christensen, Glean 49
Christensen, Peart 49
Christensen, Walt . . . . . .iv,
. 13,49,77
Clapp, Russell 89
Cole, Freda 83
Cowgitt, Wilma
Crittenden Harrington-Mac
Crittenden, Mr
Custer, Father Arnold 89
Cutler, Bob 71
Dahlgren. George
Davis, Reverend Dale . . .89
Deitz, Jack 13,15
Edens Family
Edens, Dick 69, 70,
. . . . .72, 73
Edens, Jr., Dick 69, 70,
. . . . .72, 73,
. 74
Edens, William 69-72
    Shelly Erickson 74
    Loree Edens 74
    Beth Tutt 74
Edens, Gwen 69, 70,
. . . . .72, 73
. . . .,74
Edens, Helen
Elias, Helen 69, 70,
. 71
Elhs, Norman
English, Jack
English, Susan
Erikson, Charlie 12
Flindahl, Jean 27, 87,
. 88
Friebrock, Eric 10
Friemouth, "Red"
Gates, Reverend & Mrs. .89

Gavin, Alsa F.
Gjorsund. Ermel 33
Gnad, S.S.
Gordon Family . . . . .53-55.
. 57-61,
. 72-73
Gordon, Harris L. 61
    Joyce Farney 61
    Sherry Ithal 61
    Galen 61
    Thelma 61
    Joan Edens 61
Gordon, Rt. Rev Bishop . .89
Graham, Jim 21
Greenough, Louis
Grey (Gray), Dick 7,29,
. . . . .30,35, 55
Grey, Babe
Groth, Mrs. 29,60
Hansen, "Booie" 38-40
Hansen, "Tepa" 38-41,
. . . . .83, 93
Hansen, Bert 42
Hansen, Gilbert
Hansen, Inga 38-40
Hansen, LaRene Joy
Hansea, Gerald WiJliam . .37
Harrington Family 1, 12, 13,
. . . . .55, 56,
. 69
Harringlon, Bill 14
Harrington, Jack 14
Harrington, Jane 14
Haslund, Gus 13
Haumelbacher, Mrs.
Heath, Hazel
Heddel Family 16
Heddel, Duncan 16
Heddel, Francis 16
Heddel, Peter
Hegdahl, Harry
Hegdahl, Wilda
Herbert, John
Herndon Family 16
Hewlett Family
Hewlett, Anna 93
Hewlett, Arthur 43, 93,
. 94

Hewlett, Natalie 93
High, Homer 15,87
High, Mary 87
Hillstrand, Earl 81, 49
Holmes, "Old Man" 30
James, Opal 17
James, Pete
Jensen, Jens 55
Jensen, Torvald
Johanson, Anton 90
Johnston, Reverend 89
Jones Family
Jones, Alfred 81
Jones, Paul
Katchutin, George 12
Kirsch, Ernest 70
Klockenteger, Ardis 13
Klockenteger, Arlene 13
Kohler, Rocky 7
Kohler, Mrs.
Kranich Family 76-79
Kranich, Arleen 1, 72, 75,
. . . . .76, 78-
. . . . .79, 87
Kranich, Bill 76-79
Kranich, Bob 76-79
Kranich, Eugene 31
Kranich, Ray 76-79
Lang, Charlie 12
Larson, "Cat Man"
Latham Family
Lathrop, Cap 84
Lee, Roland 35
Lenferink, Mrs. 89
Linstrang, Henry 9-11
Lipke. Adam 16
Lippincott, Mrs. 25-27
Long, Orma 12
Malaka, John
Marteeny, Paul 88
Mathews, William L.
Mauseth, Shorty 65
McCroskey, Mr. 30, 58
McCullough, Nellie 87
McDonald, Donald 30
McKenzie, Dr. Ralph 361
McLane, Enid 54,56
Miller, Charley 5, 13, 30,

Miller, Emma & George
Miller, Marlene iv
Miller, Pat
Mills, Jack 89
Minnie 9
Moore, Ken & Snooks
Moss, Brothers 48
Mover, Reverend Nelson .89
Munson Family 12
Munson, Ed (Fred) 29
Munson, Esther 13
Munson, Nellie
Munroe Turk 76
Myhill, Jackie` 73
Neilsen Family 13-22
    Stanley
    Luzadder, Susan
    Einar (Gus)
    Ema
    Frieda
    Karl
    Mabel
    Peggy
    Peter
    Samuel
    Stanley
    Starr
    William
Nimic
Nordby, Mrs. 45
Ohlsen, Henry 13, 16,
    . . . . .55, 90
Pavaloff, Francis 43
Peck, Biff 13
Pemberly Stephen
Pennock, Homer 4
Peterson, Alien v
Petersoa Jetty (Jettie) . . .v
Pratt, Sam . . . . .v, 56-58,
   87
Pratt, Thelma Hope v
Pugh, Dale 14
Rasmussen, Elmer 14, 28,
   94
Reesof, Lydia 14, 28
Richardson, Margaret . . .28, 29,
   70
Richardson, Marion 28, 29
Ridgeway, Ben

Rogers, Anita Mary
Rogers, Judy Ann
Rogers, Lawrence 39, 43
Rogers, Linda Mae
Rose, Mr. 69
Rosenberg, Karl 12, 48
Schaefer/Shaffer, Stanton v
Schoate, Vera
Scott, Ethel
Shafer, Dad 30
Sharp, Charlie 15, 54
Shelford, Tom 14,49
Shelford, Lydia 55, 76,
   87
Sholin Family 29-33
    Shirely 29-33, 83
    Ann 23-25, 30
    Bob 31
    Dale 32
    Helen 32
    Steven 32
    Shelley 32
    Losis 32

Sholin, Andrew 86
Sholin,Ed 86
Shotter, Mrs. 50
Smith, Olive 48
Smith, Myrle 88
Svedlund, Nils 13-14,27,
    . . . . .45, 50,51
Svedlund, Garron 69
Svedlund, Freddy iv
Taylor, Carl 88
Tillion,Clem 48
Umiuski, Bud 72
Waddell, Guy 55
Waddell, Jim 49, 73
Walli, Ero & Lillian 7-18
Watson, Hugh 61
Wells, Henry 87
Wendt, Ivar 82
Woodman, Oscar 63-67
    Maruie 63-67
    Sonya 67
    Kim 67
Zowistowski, Steve 52

HOMER PIONEERS